Twelve Rows Back

Twelve Rows Back

Some Mutterings from

Tom Eaton

DOUBLE
STOREY
a juta company

First published 2005 by Double Storey Books,
a division of Juta & Co. Ltd,
Mercury Crescent, Wetton, Cape Town

© 2005 Tom Eaton

ISBN 1 77013 019 5

Layout by Claudine Willatt-Bate
Printing by CTP Printers, Parow, Cape Town

For my parents, Tony and Erna, who continue to hope that one day I will be strong and brainy enough to bring in the coal; and for Gretchen, who still insists that cricket is just hitting a ball with a plank.

Back in the good old RSA

In which the SABC paints the first of many large bull's-eyes on its flabby buttocks, and I oblige.

For those who continue to bleat about unfair domination in sport, I have four letters: USSR.

Once, in a time called The Eighties, when a Ferrari was something driven by Thomas Magnum PI and Australian cricket was a howling wasteland of mullets and Village People moustaches, the Soviet Union ruled half the world.

Its athletes, potato-faced monsters captured at birth by the KGB and raised on a diet of rusty iron slabs marinated in petrol, confounded doping experts and gynaecologists from Mexico City to Moscow. They were impossibly fast, impossibly strong, and impossibly ugly. Soviet television was perpetually blurred for a reason: any close-ups would have induced national hysteria, leading to nausea, disorientation and finally death.

History has been unkind to the hard-working Soviet television producer, who has slipped into the shadow of anonymity unlike, for instance, Russian biochemical engineers who all learned Afrikaans and moved south. But that was until last Friday night. Now we know where all Russia's television experts are. They are working for SABC2's sports desk.

The national broadcaster's usual Friday night fare of wholesale slaughter was gone. In its place was something called the Presidential Sports Awards. Naturally one eagerly awaited the chance to see the State President presented with award after award for achievements in a variety of presidential sports: Eyebrow-Beetling, Laborious Joke-Telling, Prisoner-Pardoning, Virus-Vanishing. But it was not to be.

Over a soundtrack lifted straight from a Ukrainian porno film the presenter – a man with a deep inability to understand the workings of a tie – told us that we could expect some 'great spectacular moments'. These, it turned out, were endless scenes of anonymous people shuffling into a stuffy marquee, blinking into Gulag spotlights and trying to wrangle enormous ball-gowns into place, rather like trying to park the *Queen Mary* in a Portapool.

The skin-flick muzak bumped and ground on and on until finally the State President trundled into view towing a blimp that turned out to be Sports Minister Nconde Balfour. President Mbeki, groomed and gleaming as a Caramello Bear with his Condensed Milk Cousin at his side, should have been the star attraction, but Yuri in his production van outside had other ideas, focusing his cameras on empty tables, someone's hat, and a very nervous lady who turned out to be the Mistress of Ceremonies.

Apparently Yuri was also in charge of putting together the patriotic montage that flickered across our screens while the Soweto String Quartet sawed and butchered its way through the unsuspecting national anthems. The flag flapping over Madiba's beaming features was fair enough, but suddenly it all went to hell: there were helicopters, someone watering plants, a very white girl on a very white beach, a factory. Yuri, it seemed, was missing his family on the shores of Lake Baikal. Before we could get to tractor-races and games with birch branches in saunas, the montage was over and the MC was inviting the 'face of South Africa sport' to open the proceedings.

If Mr Balfour's face is that of South African sport, is it implicit that his body is likewise the incarnation of the national pastime? That might explain why we can't win anything. Unfortunately we didn't get to watch the face that launched a thousand quips for long, as Yuri, dreaming of potatoes, silenced him in mid-platitude. The MC, restraining herself with a great effort from turning into a blob of sycophantic jelly, called on 'the big man himself', and Mbeki slapped down Balfour and rose to his feet.

What he said will remain a mystery, for as he began to speak Yuri focused on Herschelle Gibbs, crouching furtively over some hors d'oeuvres. Gibbs's outfit – a shirt with a collar apparently made out of a dishtowel – should be a stern reminder to us all of the dangers inherent in letting sportsmen dress themselves. It was too awful to watch any more of.

In defence of Yuri and SABC2 it must be added that two nights later they aired an excellent interview with Robin Peterson, the young cricket all-rounder. The sound was superb, the editing crisp. Robin's hopes and dreams were probed: he says the South African camp is 'quietly confident' ahead of their first World Cup match, and he wants to score a hundred in the Final.

So the news is two months late. Who's counting anyway – right, Yuri?

Wanted: Comical Ali

Not since Cliff Saunders has a media figure been as resolutely opti-mistic about the future of the dictatorship he supports as was Chemical Ali, the Iraqi Grand Panjandrum for Hoopla, who is probably counting down the hours in his Guantánamo Bay cell until the cadres of the Grand Resistance Army of Saddam the Hirsuit storm ashore at Coney Island …

Thirty days ago nobody had heard of Mohammed Saeed al-Sahaf. Today everybody has a favourite 'Comical Ali' one-liner. The Iraqi Minister of Information has spawned a T-shirt boom, websites and fan clubs. And why wouldn't he? He is a gem, and one that South African sport badly needs.

Imagine what otherworldly observations came from the Minister during his inevitable flight to Damascus along with the rest of the Iraqi high command. 'Do not be afraid of that helicopter gunship heading for our truck, comrades, any moment now loyal peasants will annihilate it with well-aimed rocks. That is not a missile coming our way, brothers, it is a burning American airman. See how he roars past and slams into the Volvo behind us. While there is nothing to fear, I think we should entrench ourselves behind that patriotic dune over there as I think I see another burning American airman coming our way. Bugger.'

It's safe to assume that al-Sahaf's career as a Minister is over, but it is almost certain that his creative genius will not be lost to the world. At this moment head-hunters from KPMG and Microsoft are racing the Marines to the Syrian border in a desperate bid to capture the rarefied mind that steams under that little black beret. And South African sport has fumbled the ball by not being part of that race.

Instead of enlisting the services of the greatest spin-doctor since Pik Botha, our sporting leaders continue in the naïve belief that the public wants to hear the truth.

Signs of this horrible candour are everywhere. Last weekend Stormers captain told news agencies that his team 'threw away' its Super 12 match against the Queensland Reds. Good God, Corné, are you mad? Drunk on this heady mix of defeatism and honesty, coach Gert Smal weighed in with the observation that if one doesn't perform on the day 'you can be humiliated'. Oh, for two tranquilliser darts and a big black van to carry the unconscious duo away for re-education …

It could have been so lovely. With Krige and Smal chained to each other in a dank cellar under Newlands, al-Sahaf would have addressed the media. 'What appeared to be a Stormers' loss was in fact a tactical repositioning of our players. We have found glory by outsmarting the Australian invaders. Their bellies are roasting in hell.' How do you account for the score? some cynically unsporting reporters will ask. 'Naturally the score is a fabrication of the Australian media. There is no score. You are a victim of your country's obsession with scores. Do not panic. I am here. You can call me Al.'

Unfortunately celebrations of the Stormers' victory (with the customary stamping on posters of Reds players and shooting of AK-47s into the air) would have been cut short as news came in from Bangladesh that Biff Smith was blabbing about South Africa's thrashing by India.

Smith, poor misguided child that he is, was reported as saying that he got things a bit mixed up in arranging his bowling attack, and that he had been guilty of a 'tactical error' in not allowing Shaun Pollock to finish his full ten-over spell. If only al-Sahaf had been on hand to explain the real situation …

'There was no blunder. Brigadier Pollock bowled his full spell, and took 34 wickets in eleven deliveries, including three consecutive hat tricks. Field Marshal Smith distinguished himself by scoring the first triple-century in a one-day international.'

Of course it will be a major setback to our sports if we don't get Comical Ali. Sports and Recreation Minister Nconde Balfour has shown flashes of promise with some solid doublespeak and workmanlike evasion, but so far his efforts have fallen short of the mark. Witness his reaction to the news that New Zealand football wallah Charles Dempsey would not be part of the World Cup 2010 bid selection team, an all-too-frank 'Thank God' that the Kiwi was gone.

Ali would have had none of it. 'We have never lost a bid. We win every bid we attempt. As for the New Zealand aggressor, here is footage of him taken in a Baghdad prison yesterday. Pay no attention to what seems to be the Waldorf Astoria behind him. The bid-rigging aggressor has been incinerated. His belly roasts in hell.'

Much Ad Do about Nothing

In 2003 I thought advertising and those who practised it were the lowest form of human life. Since then I've met a few copywriters and an executive, and have been forced to revise that opinion. No, human life has nothing at all to do with the industry. Advertising is a moral septic tank inhabited by ticks whose only human traits are greed, vanity, ignorance and boorishness. I could have written a strongly worded letter to my local knock-and-drop, but they can't afford my kind of rates and wouldn't have given me a by-line and photograph. So I wrote a column about it instead.

Advertising works, as the poor fools who bought the new Candíce single can bear grim testimony to. Apparently South Africa's advertising industry is one of the best in the world, but frankly that doesn't mean a whole lot when you look at some of the competition. European ads are about as much fun as Finland. In China they blow up your house and imprison your only child if you don't buy Chairman Mao Democratic Synthetic Cheese.

India has a middle class greater than the entire population of the United States. That's about five taxi-loads of people heading for the Ciskei at Christmas. But this holy cash cow remains relatively elusive as the country's advertising gurus face the fact that there are fifteen times as many Indian gods as there are Indians. Pepsi and MRF may have turned Sachin Tendulkar into the God of Cover Drives, but he's still got to get in line behind Armichand the Nine-Fingered God of

Band-Aids and Chunki the Frustrated Six-Armed God of Cling-Wrap. At last, realising the impossibility of creating enthusiasm for worldly things in a culture founded on supernatural hype, the ad men get straight to the point. 'Got leprosy? Sachin is the lift you need!' For some reason the awards continue to elude New Delhi's top agencies …

Which brings us a back to South Africa and a nagging question about its ad industry: if it's so good, how does one account for the marketing campaigns of SuperSport and SAA?

The latter's sports-related adverts are merely embarrassing. Their sucks-to-you World Cup campaign could have been worse, if they'd pitched it at eight-year-olds, for example, instead of their target market, socially retarded narcissistic 10-year-olds. We'll let them get on with losing money at an astonishing rate.

But SuperSport should know better. Actually that's not true. It has done nothing in its history to dissuade one from thinking that its marketing department is staffed by a team of the above-mentioned pre-teens, a festering sludge of human detritus incapable of higher reason, with fingers wedged far up nostrils and tongues lolling in idiot glee. These are, after all, the people that used to advertise Test cricket with images of batsmen being felled by bouncers, intercut with charming footage of a skull on a stick being shattered by a cricket ball.

Apparently some senior marketing exec finally tore himself away from his ball pond and Batman comics and told his lackeys to get some culture, resulting in a shift away from the obvious analogies of tribal bloodshed to the even more obvious analogies of modern warfare. What Super 12 rugby has to do with the battle for Iwo Jima in World War Two is beyond me, but that campaign's most famous image – the raising of a flag by marines – has been transplanted onto South Africa's screens and broadsheets in a misguided attempt at martial gong-banging. Unfortunately the final result – six or seven sweaty blokes in tiny shorts grasping at a big pole – looks more homoerotic than heroic.

Tennis, too, has been subjected by SuperSport to the Saving Private Ryan treatment. While one can just see the faintest connection between war and playing Under-13 rugby (moments of absolute terror, eternities of deathly boredom), watching Agassi drill a forehand down the line to the sound of machine-gun fire is an astonishing outing into the mind of the lowest common denominator. Grim sweaty faces are shown as the narrator makes some half-arsed attempt at sounding like Winston Churchill, and we're supposed to believe that Lleyton Hewitt is going through hell on earth, a trial by hot lead, instead of prancing about on a big flat lawn, being paid a zillion bucks for playing a game.

All this might explain why SuperSport is not covering the current Test series in Bangladesh: its marketing monkeys couldn't think of an appropriate war to doll up. It's a tricky one, to be sure. They needed a war in which a superpower went and smashed up a small Asian country. Vietnam! But that would require Biff Smith's players to stay there for two years, slowly losing players to venereal disease and groin strains before a final hard-fought defensive draw at Chittagong and a low-key return to Johannesburg International Airport. And to be realistic, if they showed scenes of Jacques Rudolph clubbing baby harp seals or Shaun Pollock lighting up his flame-thrower outside a convent, it still wouldn't come close to the reality of the current mismatch over there.

War is hell. SuperSport ads are worse.

The big question

This one goes out to my homies in the Under-15 table-tennis team of 1992, that band of brothers who kept their swagger and fighter-jock esprit secret behind braces and asthma pumps, and whose nerveless duels on the table of dreams will forever be their secret preserve, unknown and unheralded by those mediocre masses who blindly support 'real' sports …

What is sport, and who decides what counts as a sport? High-school coaches will tell you that sport is fun, as they nick the heels of weeping 13-year-olds with a well-oiled sjambok called Wagter. For Australian ranchers there's nothing better than downing a pint of antifreeze and then going after 'roos with a bow and fiery arrows. Chinese mystics get their sporting kicks on a Saturday afternoon by stopping their hearts and letting moss grow all over them. It all seems fairly relative.

Perhaps it is safe to suggest that to qualify as a sport an activity must have some entertainment value. But that disqualifies anything involving the Cats and the Stormers. Chess is a case in point. Is it a sport or a psychosis? Certainly its greatest players behave like sportsmen, as any hotel maid who has ever had to clean up after Bobby Fischer knows. In fact it is likely that apart from harbouring paranoid fantasies about Commie Republicans in black helicopters, Bobby also used to bang his head against lockers to psych himself up before a crunch match. It's just hard to take something seriously as a sport when the highlights package shows seven hours of meditation, interspersed with the players taking turns to bang triumphantly on the snooze button of a little alarm clock next to the board.

But perhaps we can't judge an activity on its value as a spectacle. For example, nobody watches fox-hunting, yet its participants believe that it is a sport. This is because they forgot to ask the fox what he felt about the whole thing. Of course Rupert and Arabella, astride Pongo and Theseus, insist that they are giving the beastie a sporting chance. You know, the way laser-guided cluster bombs give one a sporting chance. But honestly, what kind of event is based on blood and pain, in which a large group of inbreeders massacre a tiny, helpless target? Apart from any match involving the Cats?

Why is a marathon considered a sport while hanging wet laundry on a rotating line is not? Both leave one emotionally and psychologically spent, muscles stretched beyond breaking point. Both celebrate humankind's triumph over impossible odds. Both involve damp underwear. And if curling continues to blight the winter Olympics, in all fairness one has to allow casserole-dish-scrubbing, window-squeegeeing and cat-delousing to turn professional.

Cheerleading has become an officially recognised sport in the United States, which means that if you go to a pro basketball game over there you will at least be watching one real sport, at half-time. Only a civilisation capable of producing Barbra Streisand and *Survivor Thailand* could have thought it would be a good idea to invent a sport in which freaks try to put a big ball through a hoop. Who came up with basketball? Was he at the circus, watching Shaqeel the Flaming Seal jump through a hoop with a second left on the clock? One can understand the symbolic history of most other sports – one runs across a line to symbolise completion, one hits a ball with a modified plank because international law prohibits one from hitting necks with a modified chain-saw – but what possible symbolism could there be in basketball? Posting letters? Collecting eggs? Certainly the most enjoyable basketball games are those played by lab rats in small glass tanks, when each basket is rewarded with a crouton. Now that's a sport.

Still, basketball looks like quantum physics next to synchronised swimming, a sport based on the belief that six legs, wobbling about in the air and looking every inch like the morning after on the *Titanic*, will create the illusion of balletic grace and poise. However, no one has told these soggy sugarplum fairies that water is transparent and we can see their suffering little faces and thrashing little arms down there as they desperately fight off the encroaching Kreepy-Krauly.

There seems to be only one solution that will satisfy everyone: all human endeavour must be declared sport, and we can all take pride in being champions. Next time you need to bath the dog, take a moment, gather yourself: it'll be tough, but if you dig deep, find that extra 10 per cent to take you up to 120 per cent and push through the pain barrier, you will emerge triumphant, with a clean dog and the heady scent of victory that is the domain of the champion.

Separate Development

Sports development, correctly pronounced 'spots divlorpment', is a noble endeavour, rather like putting a man on the moon. And like putting a man on the moon it is staggeringly expensive, immensely time-consuming, potentially fatal, and is responsible for the release of gigantic volumes of hot air.

How do pole-vaulters do it the first time? Do they have the pole glued to their hands before being shot out of a small cannon to give them a taste of the glamorous new life that awaits them? We all know that when you take a Ferrari Formula One car past 300 kph the galaxy splinters into a zillion little streaks that smear back over your window while Chewbacca in the co-pilot seat makes irate seal noises. But how does one do that the first time? Who takes you by the hand and teaches you to do the impossible?

The answer to this question, as to so many others, is sports clinics. We've all seen them on dusty fields, a scene straight out of *Lord of the Flies*. So many children, so few straitjackets. Observe one of these apocalyptic marshalling yards and one will understand that 'clinic' is an apt description: the dearth of equipment and motivated staff is the sporting equivalent of a caravan in the bundu stocked with one rusty hypodermic and roll of duct tape. No one actually dies, but no one's really cured either.

It seems that once one has been stabilised at the clinic, one is ready to go to sports hospital. These are huge buildings where visitors pay ridiculous amounts to gain entrance and then bleed on the floor, like the FNB Stadium after a vibrant crowd has been too vibrant. And of course there are sports hospices too, where has-been players go to end it all. Sometimes at night, if you listen very carefully, you can hear the iron-lung machines inside Ellis Park.

Allegedly there is method to the madness of sports clinics. As the Sports Ministry handbook says, 'Wherever two or more of you are gathered together in my name, hitting Slazballs through minibus windows, there you shall find Development.' For you see, Development is that silver bullet that will see us wiping out the Aussies at cricket and rugby, wiping out the Yanks at track and field, wiping out the Finns at long-distance ski-trekking and glacier-hurdling. And as the handbook says, if Development is with, who can be against us?

One of the perks of Development in the new South Africa is that all children, irrespective of colour or creed, can now spend their free time stubbing their toes on half-bricks in the veld while they shuttle between orange plastic cones. Of course if any of them plan to play Test cricket in India one day they must be entirely familiar with half-bricks, stun grenades, Molotov cocktails and small burning motorcycles, all of which generally cascade over the fence and onto deep fine leg at Eden Gardens. But it seems that the rest of the children, dodging their cones, learn more about stoicism and heatstroke than sport.

When you get right down to it, ignoring the hoopla about equality and camaraderie, development is deeply discriminatory in this country. When was the last time you saw a bus full of young development quail-shooters heading off with a Venter trailer full of hounds and elderly Scottish beaters? And fly-fishing: why are the banks of our major rivers not packed with thousands of tiny children in rubber pants sponsored by Doom?

The biggest travesty of Development is fox-hunting, a sport so badly neglected by the Sports Ministry that it is not even practised in this country. Excuses are made by Ministry spokespeople: the foxes have all been stolen, they were stinky anyway, you can't hit one with an AK once it's more than twenty yards away, etc. South Africa's handful of dedicated fox-hunters have been patient for years, making do with saddling up their bicycles and tearing off across the Karoo after dassies, but their patience cannot last forever, and when they snap, don't be surprised if we see a dramatic upturn in corgi kidnappings.

Perhaps it's time to view Development more holistically, to embrace more than just herds of children. Take for instance street racers. These are experts in their sport, men who have dedicated their lives to turning Ford Cortinas into manned missiles and who possess the ancient lore of how to do a proper donut without bursting their Bridgestones. That takes time and dedication, and yet the Development programme has ignored them. This is a real pity, as I firmly believe that with a lot of love and effort they could be trained to speak and walk upright, perhaps even to read large-print books with lots of pictures. I have a dream …

Motoring in the Mother City

People often ask me why I hate Port Elizabeth and East London so much. Please. That's like asking why I hate Switzerland. As for this piece, I fax it to Bernie once a month but his people still haven't called my people, and I have to consider the possibility that appending a cheery 'Jou ma se Porsche' to my faxes hasn't been the best idea.

Last weekend Prince Rainier (brother of Drizzly, son of Slightly Overcast Grimaldi) shook the hand of some South American bloke who wasn't Michael Schumacher, and the Monaco Grand Prix was over. No more glamour for a whole year, sighed Bernie Ecclestone on Monday morning, brushing his teeth with diamond dust. In Monaco's massive underground jails the thousands of vagrants and Americans rounded up by the police before the race were released with a warning beating and told to get some class before being issued with pictures of Liberace and Cher to model themselves on.

But Monaco isn't all it's cracked up to be. Sure, there's lots of money, but there's lots of money in Switzerland too and nobody in their right mind lives in that hellhole. The local ad execs, all tax fugitives from Germany, have done wonders with the place, but if 'Monte Carlo' sounds très chic, when the dentures come out at the end of the day it still just means 'Charles Mountain'. Mount Chucky. Chuckberg.

And those royals who run the place aren't fooling anyone either. They might marry Hollywood aristocracy and play bumper-boats in the harbour, but money can't buy you class and history will remember them for what they are: circus freaks. Seriously, what sort of surname is Grimaldi? Would you genuflect before a King Grimaldi, or expect to see him blinking a third eye in the middle of his forehead while he plays a banjo in a peepshow? The prosecution rests.

Our own ageing Prince – the man who would be king were it not for that pesky Mandela fellow – has declared this to be the African century, and if Africa is to become a player, Bernie needs to get out of his jacuzzi filled with Château-Rothschild '29 and hop a flight to Chwannisbeg to scope out the potential for a new South African Grand Prix.

Of course we've had them before. Who will ever forget Williams Renault world champion Nigel Mansell crossing the line under a piece of cardboard reading 'My Mate Nige', parking his car between some blackjacks on the least cracked bits of concrete, and spraying J.C. le Roux all over the thirteen spectators and a stray dog? But a new century needs a new race, and most importantly it needs a new Monaco.

Johannesburg would be a strong contender: its denizens already wear leopard-print jeans and too much gold jewellery, and most have become accustomed to cars travelling at over 300 kph along its streets. But sponsors might not take kindly to Kimmi Raikkonen's McLaren being overtaken by a taxi called 'Dreamlover' containing seventeen people, a primus stove and a goat.

Pretoria has wide roads and the old-world charm of, say, Stonehenge, but there are all those one-ways. Durban would be fairly picturesque, and it has a harbour for the odd spectacular prang, but they don't run Grands Prix in rainforests for a reason: the cars explode while idling on the grid, Bernie sweats into his caviar, and pit-crews have to fight leeches and anacondas while waiting for their man to come in. No one is yet able to tell Port Elizabeth and East London apart, and both are indistinguishable from Khabarovsk-am-Kray, a small grey concrete mining town in eastern Siberia, so perhaps not quite enough glamour there ...

No, it's going to have to be Cape Town. Schumacher and Raikonen touching wheels on the Camps Bay beachfront; the scream of monstrous engines ripping through Clifton; the nausea-inducing on-board footage as Jacques Villeneuve heads down Kloof Nek at 240 kph before wrapping his BAR around a pine-tree. It will be quite magnificent. Of course Juan Montoya's temper might get somewhat frayed as he turns into the pit lane and is offered fifty black refuse bags for R9.99, and garage crews could also take strain from helpful blokes who dance out into oncoming traffic, pointing and whistling at an open spot before demanding money. The drivers' argument – that they will only be stopping for around 7.2 seconds – falls on deaf ears.

There's always the danger of bergie-strike (a bottle of meths can do fearful things to a Ferrari engine), and then there is the south-easter: it wouldn't do to have Jenson Button blown into the Atlantic, the British High Commission adding 'wind' to its tome of warnings for tourists, a list that already includes sunburn, penguins, locals with no teeth, and Heinz Winkler.

But I have faith in Bernie, because Bernie, just like life in Jurassic Park, will find a way.

Sport by the book

In which another publisher rejects Eaton's novel, forcing him to vent his spleen on the less verbose and more commercial.

'Write without pay until somebody offers to pay you,' said Mark Twain to all aspiring writers. 'If nobody offers within three years, sawing wood is what you were intended for.' But what happens when some wretched specimen, sawmill-fodder to his core, is offered a pile of cash to write his autobiography?

Impossible, you say. Why would we want to lift the lid on the daily grind of being a wood-chipper? Why would we possibly be interested in hearing the thoughts of someone who left school at fifteen and who sweats and grunts for a living?

And yet walk into any bookshop and there is a shelf bulging with such offerings. All have titles that are a permutation of *In My Own Words*, one of the great ironies of publishing if one looks behind the curtain where ghost-writers pound away, manacled to word-processors and clutching *The Oxford Dictionary of Awful Puns*. Somewhere along the line the myth that writers are by definition interesting people has been grafted to the myth that celebrities are by definition interesting people, and the result, in all its 700-page splendour, a literary form of crotch-rot, is the autobiography of the sportsman.

Expecting a footballer to express in writing a series of engaging anecdotes, bound together by an inevitable message of moral upliftment and hope for the future, is like expecting the Pope to pop his Popemobile into fifth and grease Schumacher on the final corner at Imola, taking victory in a blur of white robes and flailing rosaries. It's just not worth waiting for.

Yet agents and publishers persist. About five years ago a young South African star (I drop no names, unlike some of the more desperate biographers about) was being interviewed over the phone by a colleague of mine. Standard stuff: favourite colour, favourite film, the usual banalities that fill the nebulous rear ends of magazines. The young star was barely verbal, let alone literate, but the telling moment came when he was asked his favourite food. There was a sniff, a pause, and then a yell. 'Mommy!' he called into the depths of his ancestral home. 'Mommy, what's my favourite food?' 'Chicken!' came the reply. Another sniff. 'Chicken,' said the star. Two months later his autobiography appeared. There were plenty of pictures, and the font was very large ...

Which is not to say that some sportobiographies aren't entertaining. Lance Armstrong, for instance, has become the Norman Mailer of sweaty undies. Likewise every so often a rangy loner climbs a mountain, runs out of rope and oxygen, has to eat his Sherpa (cooked over a cigarette lighter), uses up the entire fuel budget of the Nepalese air force as he is helicoptered to safety, and then writes a book called *I Fought Death and Won*. These accounts are intended as disturbing insights into the dark spaces of the human mind but invariably come across like rough drafts of Biggles novels, which makes them far more interesting than if they had been well written.

Of course the real question is: why should we read books by sportsmen when they don't read books by real authors? In another *Favourites* quiz a senior member of the South African cricket team announced that the last book he'd read was 'Janet and John' in Grade Three. He was serious, and proud of the fact. Surely the handlers of our national team must cringe when players, asked what their favourite novel is, name *Sports Illustrated*? Or are the administrators too busy enjoying the earthy realism and bold narrative structure of *Archie at Riverdale High*?

The Art of War, a book almost as boring as the people who read it, has managed to qualify as a sports tome. Long the instruction manual of businessmen who have used its pseudo-mystical hyper-macho claptrap as justification for the spiritual decrepitude their profession requires, it now lies on the gold-plated bedside tables of golfers the world over.

At least this was written by an Oriental gent well into his career as, er, a military artiste. Which is more than can be said of the new breed of autobiographies, appearing between three weeks and a month into the career of a young star. One can understand camel jockeys writing their memoirs when they turn nine – their careers are effectively over – but the story of cricketer Paul Adams's life hit the shelves when that life had barely spanned eighteen years. Can we expect a sequel? *The First Quarter-Century*?

I'm off to write my memoirs.

O2B@LS

The modern reader must forgive the archaic tone of this piece, written as it was all the way back in June 2003. According to Nokia's historian, cellphones of this era were still only able to send text messages and perform limited household chores. She was going to MMS me more data, but my phone has developed a paranoid ennui, manifesting as passive-aggression, which makes dealing with it very unpleasant. From time to time I buy it gifts, but it taunts me when I do, saying I'm patronising it instead of being honest and admitting that I pity it for not being human. This week it has decided it is fat and hideous, and now refuses to ring in public.

What would history have looked like had cellphones – and more specifically SMSs – been around to grease the wheels of communication? Would Mrs Ulysses have been spared a decade of pining if her phone had bleeped and revealed a note from hubby? 'Will b late for supr, we R N big woodn horse outside Troy + then taking scenic way home. XXX U.'

Certainly the great orators and poets of the world would have been able to get their message across more quickly (depending on network availability), and the Bard, Wilm Shkspr, needn't have bothered with ink, sealing wax and stamps when he asked, 'shl i compar the 2 a sumerz da?' Christian missionaries would never have had to get off the riverboat, instead tapping away on their keypads while playing shuffle-board: '+ god cre8d the hevn + the erth.' Franklin D Roosevelt and Martin Luther King could have saved themselves the nasty throat strains they picked up when they cried, 'We hav 0 2 fear but fear itslf' and 'Free @ last! Thnk god almIT, free @ last!'

Of course the advent of SMSs has underlined the fact that not everybody should be given a voice. Some people should not say anything, ever. They should be locked in a storm-water drain and sterilised. And they should not be allowed to watch rugby.

M-Net has not conquered all of Gaul just yet. A hardened few have managed to resist the incandescent gleam of Peter Ndoro's immense polished forehead and the anaesthetising speech impediments of Marius Roberts, and have to make alternative arrangements to watch rugby tests. For this band SABC2 offers a programme called *Rugga as Live as Budgets Allow Hence a Time Delay of Around Two Hours*. Once M-Net has feasted on the live spectacle, it tosses the lukewarm carcass of the match to the national broadcaster, where Gerald de Kock battles to breathe some life into the poor thing, the voice of a thousand men around the country chanting the mantra, 'If you know who won, don't say a bloody word because I'm still watching.'

Rugga Previously Live would be almost watchable if it had not decided to parade, in an endless litany of illiteracy and oafishness, the SMSs of the nation across the screen during Saturday's match at Ellis Park. Slakkie from Benoni thinks anyone who are not a Joost supporter are stupit. Sue-Anne from Durbs and her posse think that André Snyman has a hot bum, tee hee. These are fictional examples, but they're poetry next to some of the stuff that dribbled across our consciousness for most of the match. O2BNLA, where people raised on vanity plates know how to be succint.

Perhaps it was part of some kind of desperate community-building exercise. Certainly SABC3's sports desk seems to be going that route, if Sunday night's coverage of the Canadian Grand Prix is anything to go by. The eternally unflappable Bob Mabena and Graham Duxbury were crouched as usual over a Styrofoam desk, salivating in anticipation over the start of the race (which in Real Time had began 90 minutes previously but was still a good half-hour away in Kempton Park Time). By the way, if the East German entrants in the Eurovision Song Contest of 1982 are looking for their set, tell them to call the SABC.

That Duxbury brought along his young son to add to the homely feel of the show was just bearable, even if the tiny youth did stumble through a camera-shy spiel about his tennis career and Schumacher's chances, while who knows what happened in Montreal. But the most bizarre was still in store. As the crucial second round of pit stops loomed nearer and Bob announced that 'We're almost ready to cross over for the start' (what a relief that must have been to Bernie Ecclestone, waiting on tenterhooks in Canada for news of SABC's linkup), Duxbury revealed that he had been at the Monaco Grand Prix and had brought along his holiday snaps.

'This is me in the tunnel, sorry it's a bit dark,' he said. 'And that blur there, no, just there, in the corner, behind the Shell billboard, no, there … yes, that's the bumper of David Coulthard's back-up car. And this is Michael Schumacher's manager's shoe, and here's a great group of South Africans I met over there.' Ten out-of-focus blokes clutching Castles in a small clinical hotel room: the glamour of Monaco. Bob was smiling, but he didn't know why. Neither did we.

Sisters aren't doing it for themselves

Again this Switzerland. It haunts me like a white whale. It wants to chew off my leg with its cuckoo-clock teeth, it wants to drown me in its chocolate maw. At least Roger Federer turned out to be half South African, which presumably means his yodelling is tinged with nostalgia for the bosveld, and his morning constitutional cheese is dipped in chutney.

Roger Federer is the first Swiss man to win Wimbledon. He is also the first Swiss man to say thank you, to smile, and to have a pretty girlfriend. The chocolate tycoons of Geneva are lining up to use him as their poster boy. Well, they would be if he didn't have that ponytail: for wealth and stability Switzerland pays a cruel price in fashion, being eternally on the cusp of the 1983 Winter Season.

Despite his Wimbledon triumph, Roger has kept a low profile and remains something of a mystery. Does he use conditioner on his ponytail to get that bounce and body? Can he yodel? We just don't know. But perhaps the most important question is this: how on earth did he get to the pinnacle of tennis without a tennis-playing brother to drive him to new heights of skill?

Papa Williams, the ringmaster patriarch responsible for Venus and Serena, has convinced us that, like Sonny and Cher, his gals just aren't the same when they're apart. Doe-eyed knock-kneed Venus needs the odd whuppin' by her ripped younger sis, and Serena, packing all the grace and finesse of a cluster bomb, benefits in turn by being reminded that power isn't everything.

That's the theory. Of course, as anyone who has ever seen carpet-bombing in action knows, power *is* everything, especially when your opponent has her abs strapped up for dear life. Younger sis thumped older sis, and then tied a knot in a steel bar because she was still feeling a little punchy. These three-setters just don't satisfy a girl like they used to.

So what happens now in Chez Williams? Has Venus been grounded? 'And you'll stay up there until you beat your sister in a Grand Slam event!' Slam. One can only imagine the little notes written on Hello Kitty stationery, left under Venus' pillow: 'Dere Venus, ah'm bedder n you. Ah wurn Wimbldin. You didn't. Ha ha ha ha. XXX S.' Tears and tantrums, Froot Loops flicked at each other over the breakfast table until Papa Williams reaches for his lunging-rein …

But at least Venus is still, at very least, the second-best player in the world. Her time will come. Consider then the awful position of being an untalented sibling, one nevertheless intent on becoming a star. Is there a third Williams sister, Afrodite, chained to a boiler somewhere in the house, howling for her tennis racquet as her inch-thick bifocals steam up?

Of course we only hear about the successful sporting siblings. There is a third Waugh in Australia, who averages around 15 in backyard Tests with a plank and Slazball. At last sighting he bore quite a resemblance to Steven and Mark, but that was before he was bricked up in a cellar for the sake of cricketing symmetry. Likewise it is possible that there was a third Pollock brother in the Sixties, puny of limb and blind as a mole, who was sold to travelling gypsies when he insisted on a holding a bat upside down.

Ralf Schumacher has started winning Grands Prix, but he has surely reconciled himself to the fact that he will never be as good as Michael. Somehow one imagines that earning the GDP of sub-Saharan Africa every month has softened the blow. The difference between a zillion bucks and a billion bucks is only truly understood by lawyers and mathematicians anyway: you can't spend either amount, so why let brotherly rivalry sour a nice fraternal dip in the Lear Jet's hot-tub? Still, there must be nights when Ralf writhes about under his racing-car-motif duvet, dreaming about being trapped behind the wheel of a donkey cart as Michael fishtails over the horizon in a Ferrari spewing wads of cash out of the exhaust.

Which brings us back to the future of Roger, trying to jam his winner's tray into a safety-deposit box in Zurich. Sure, he has a glorious cross-court backhand, and yes, he has his temper under control, but if he wants to stay on top of the pile he needs to find a sibling fast. Maybe Martina Hingis. The Swiss are all related anyway. Of course Martina's mother-ship might come for her any day, drawn towards our solar system by the huge radio impulses pumped out of the dome behind her monstrous forehead. Roger had best make hay.

They don't play golf like
they used to ...

If ye find a scarred Ping at the Rondebosch Golf Course, marked wi' 'Tom's Ball', I'll gi' ye a cent fer 'im. Or a smart cuff fer waitin' t'ree bluidy years afore returning me property tae me. Bluidy cheek.

Anyone who has ever taken up an iron and swung vainly at that infinitesimally tiny ball will know that golf was invented by dour unrelenting Puritan masochists to remind themselves of the awfulness of life and the pointlessness of endeavour. Professional golfers, delusional Tinkerbells one and all, talk about motivation and achievement and satisfaction, and have thus failed utterly to understand the soul of golf. For golf, like northern Scotland on a windy day, is Purgatory.

Watching the British Open meander along in all its bleak misery, one had to wonder what the locals think. Not the convivial laddies in the commentary box, burring away to each other in half-whispers about the cracking tea they had yesterday, but the woolly Jocks skulking lugubriously beyond the television vans, alternately stroking a single niblick and a lame blind Border collie. What does old Fergus, caddie to the stars of the 1930s, think of this modern stuff?

For starters he thinks the prize money on offer is an obscenity. When he was lad, back in the seventeenth century, they used to have to play thirty-six holes a day for a lump of coal if they were lucky. And if they're going to be throwing about millions of British pounds, at least make it a useful amount, enough to buy a tropical island replete with dusky princesses and some pork chops for the dog.

Then there's the weather. The Scots have seventeen different words for rain, but somehow the nuances have been forgotten with all this golf being played in New Mexico and California. Fergus points out the difference between driving rainy horizontal sleet and sleety horizontal driving rain. The former is fine for a short game, wedges and the like, while the latter is excellent for the long irons, bedding down one's ball nice and snug in the sodden sea-grass so it doesn't bound along into the raging North Sea. Not that that's an impossible lie, mind you: old Wallace once managed a triple bogey after he refused to lose his ball (the wee bastards cost three pence, you know!) and five-putted standing chest-deep in brine.

Aye, golf in winter has its own charms, like sending the beastie (either a dog or young Hamish the blacksmith's boy) tunnelling through snowdrifts after a ball, or skipping a drive off an ice-sheet to get an extra fifty yards of distance. But then these modern milksops wouldn't know about that, the way they rush to the aerodrome and board their private monoplanes at the first hint of a chill in the air.

The crowds that come to watch have changed over the years. In the glory days your village would come and walk beside you, hurling cheery abuse and bracing obscenities to keep your mind focused. Today it's all Americans with potato-faces and expensive clothes, trampling about the greens in their huge lumberjack boots. Next thing they'll spray the out-of-bounds area with Agent Orange to make the walk less demanding.

And speaking of which, have you seen the clubs the laddies use nowadays? Monstrous great blobs, fire a ball clear to Cork. That Woods boy wouldn't be half so proud of himself if he had a bag like they played with in the old days: a niblick, a putter, a shovel for snow and coal, one spare ball (the wee bastards cost three pence, you know!) and a change of socks for when you have to putt in the ocean. If the wife had won at the bingo or the welfare cheque had come, a fellow might also pack a smoked sardine to chew on later in the afternoon, but wrapped in newspaper because nobody likes a show-off.

But perhaps the greatest abomination of modern golf, says Fergus, is the winner's speech. There he goes, this new Yank who isn't Woods, thanking this and thanking that, praising his fellow players, talking up Scotland as if we bloody need talking up, as if we're Nebraska or New Hampshire or one of those other blighted American hellholes. Why can't a fellow be honest when he wins the Open? Why can't he say, 'I don't trust your dodgy southern banks, I'll take cash, all in tenners' and then give the losers a right rollicking, maybe show them the finger or lift the kilt and moon them?

It's enough to make a lad ill. Luckily the Missis won at the bingo so Fergus can chew on his smoked sardine as he starts the long walk home.

Goodnight, sweet princes

Space constraints and a growing impatience with my inability to be succinct about anything led to 'Mail&Guardian' subs taking a machete to my slander of George Lucas, Oprah, and our weapons-procuring patriots. Just as well – one doesn't want to be sued by the Queen of Talk and the King of Drek. Luckily Double Storey have more paper and bigger litigation budgets. Right guys? Guys? Guys?

Can entertainment be measured? It certainly seems tricky in a world in which George Lucas and Oprah – jointly responsible for doubling the amount of schlock currently swilling about – were the two highest-earning 'personalities' of last year. (Naturally I use this term in its most loose American sense.)

Indeed, the couple responsible for Jar Jar Binks and Dr Phil (the one is a creepy-looking humanoid with an irritating speech impediment and bulgy eyes, the other featured in *Star Wars 4*) took home a combined $350 million last year. Of course in SANDF terms that is a drop in the corvette-clogged ocean, barely enough to pay for spare ejector seats on a Swedish fighter jet, but it has certainly kept George in hair-spray, and even those most ardent fans of Oprah are starting to suspect that her appearance on the cover of every issue of *O Magazine* might not have been a cost-cutting tactic as originally thought.

But bottom lines – and specifically those in sports – don't always provide a real measure of how much bang audiences have got for their buck. For instance it seems reasonable to suggest that most of the people who go to watch cricket Tests at Bloemfontein's Goodyear Park are being entertained, yet when the gate takings from all five days add up to R39.50, it's hard to be sure.

Sports broadcasters like SuperSport and Sky Sports (the most convincing arguments yet for eugenics) encourage those viewers not yet suffering brain haemorrhages to believe that when crowds of people surge in unison off their seats or chant along to the monosyllabic musical flatulence of Right Said Fred, those crowds of people are undergoing Entertainment. In the world of the sports broadcaster, entertainment is measured in decibels and degrees of depravity: Indians igniting a cricket stadium or South Africans going at each other with bottles and chairs at a soccer stadium are simply reflecting their love of the game and the vibrancy of the human spirit, albeit with unnecessary zeal.

All of which has relegated into obscurity the notion that entertainment is a form or relaxation, a way of getting away from things like smouldering stadiums and concussed Amakhosi. For most sports fans, sleep is something they do between spurts of work that allow them to pay for their satellite dishes, and once this aim is achieved it becomes an irritating intruder, kept at bay with Red Bulls and *Sokkie Dans Treffers* set on repeat.

If only they knew, these red-eyed twitchy slaves to novelty, of the delights that await those who are willing to surrender to sleep, to realise that sport and shuteye can be combined in the most decadent of entertainments.

Take for example BBC radio's Test Match Special, found in the murky middle regions of the South African FM dial. Those not yet fallen under its soporific spell might imagine they have stumbled into an AGM of the Royal Society for the Preservation of Cracking Watercress Sandwiches, an impression encouraged by Henry Blofeld, a commentator of such exaggerated eloquence and panache that all parodies are rendered dull by comparison. Blowers, Aggers, Bumble, the unfortunate lass known only as Shilpa who is sent to enquire after the state of Darren Gough's blisters, all combine in a murmuring spell quite impossible to resist. Nothing better illustrated the length and solidity of Graeme Smith's monumental effort at Edgbaston than drifting off during a mellifluous Jonathan Agnew spell of commentary and waking up two hours later to Blowers describing a seagull, with Smith still undefeated. Short of snoozing under a newspaper in the shade of an oak tree, sport simply cannot be any more soothing than this.

The TMS crew are in a wonderful barbiturate class of their own, but there are others for the determined sports sleeper. Now that Murray Walker has retired to torture his cat with malapropisms, Formula One races offer the chance to drift off to the whine of Martin Brundle, whose voice, despite having the plaintive air of a retriever left in the rain overnight, combines with the ambient racket in a lullaby that is almost irresistible on a Sunday afternoon.

South African commentators, still labouring under the misapprehension that they are trying to rouse their audience, continue dutifully to talk about sport, sport, and only sport. Those, uh, like, uh, Peter Davies who are, uh, employed as professional speakers because they make everyone else feel like orators, have potential as sleeptalkers, but for entirely the wrong reason.

So roll on the second Test and the sandmen of the Beeb.

What's left when everything's all right?

When I fall into a combine harvester, don't say I never saw it coming ...

What did Joan of Arc and John McEnroe have in common? Apart from 365 bad hair days a year. An overwhelming desire to kill Englishmen who disagreed with them? We don't know if Ms of Arc was also prone to blurting out 'You cannot be serious!' while cleaving British pates, but history does tell us that when her occupation of Caens was doubted, she responded by flinging her sword to the ground and screaming 'I was in! I was in!'

Certainly both had a burning ambition to light a fire under the establishment, Joan's backfiring somewhat nastily. But more importantly they were members of the world's most magnificent minority, a club that includes Leonardo da Vinci, Michelangelo, Picasso, Beethoven, Einstein and Bart Simpson. These giants of civilisation have horrible handwriting, are unable to cut paper in a straight line, and live on average almost a decade less than those who do not share their glorious gift. Simply put, they are left-handers.

Lefties have a grand tradition of breezing into sport and making it all look terribly simple. McEnroe, to many the greatest tennis player of all time, seems a veritable bridesmaid next to über-southpaw Martina Navratilova, and in the category of swinging chunks of wood at little leather balls the names of Babe Ruth, 'Shoeless' Joe Jackson, Graeme Pollock, Gary Sobers and Brian Lara head a list that includes Adam Gilchrist, Matthew Hayden, Lance Klusener and now Graeme Smith.

England's cricketers are no doubt making their own comparisons to two fairly infamous sinistrals, namely the Boston Strangler and Jack the Ripper, and whatever the result of the current Test series, England's post-mortem will not be a pretty sight, with the careers of various lionhearted bowlers smeared all over Smith's glinting blade.

As a left-hander myself it is tempting to suggest a parallel between enlightenment, sophistication and handsomeness on the one hand and left-handedness on the other; but one must be modest and concede that 90 per cent of the world's population is probably good for something, even if that something has not yet been revealed.

Right-handers do manage admirably in some arenas. Like shaking hands, for example, or saluting fascist dictators; but in sport the best they can hope for is a grudging egalitarianism between the two halves of their bodies. Which is often a good thing: Australian megatadpole Ian Thorpe would lose precious seconds should he ever veer wildly to port, his over-developed left-arm sending him whirling like a rubber-clad ferry wheel across the width of the pool.

Likewise Michael Schumacher would wind up as a Ferrari-red mist over all over the grandstands if a dominant left hand gave too great a twitch. But luckily Schumacher and all the right-handers of Formula One benefit from yet another anti-left conspiracy, with just two out of sixteen circuits featuring anticlockwise races. Right-hand hairpins, scissors, fountain pens, fish knives: so many obstacles stand in the way of the lefty and yet still he triumphs. Imagine how far Neil Armstrong and Buzz Aldrin – both southpaws – could have gone if Apollo 11 hadn't had its windscreen-wiper control switched round with its indicator lever.

Right-handers invariably have the last laugh, if for no other reason than that they generally outlive lefties: James Anderson might have looked like a bloke chucking custard pies at a brick wall in the first two Tests, but in sixty years he'll be able to mop the drool off his bib and have the satisfaction of knowing those monsters Smith, Kirsten and Rudolph are six feet under.

The statisticians suggest that left-handers have a lower life expectancy because of something called 'industrial accidents', a euphemism for a spectacular orgy of misfortune in dog-food factories and sawmills the world over. Likewise, only left-handers will ever know the adrenaline rush of firing a pistol and having a red-hot .45 cartridge ejected straight at their right eye. But perhaps it's much more simple, especially in sports: when it's all so easy and you've achieved everything, what's left to live for? Old age homes where the soupspoon is the wrong way round and the nail scissors don't work left to right? We'll take the sweet hereafter, thanks.

Baby, it's cold out there

Tall and tanned and brown and lovely, the girl from Helsinki goes walking …

Some weeks ago the Springbok rugby team swept into the little hamlet of Ceres to shoot a television advertisement for the World Cup, which is apparently happening quite soon. The action was standard stuff, *Saving Private Ryan* in white shorts, and then they signed some balls, piled into the bus and burnt rubber back to the big smoke.

Why the speedy retreat? It's possible somebody suggested a friendly match against the Charlie Hofmeyr High 1st XV, and it was deemed not in the national interest to have a barefoot 17-year-old backline frolic to three tries and a drop goal against the Boks. Or maybe the titanium rivets holding Corné Krige together needed tweaking and he'd left his ratchet set back in Cape Town.

But it seems far more likely that the lads were sensing a nip in the air. Watch the advertisement closely when it airs, and peeping out from behind Lawrence Sephaka's bottom you will see barren reddish mountains and green Koue Bokkeveld grass: you will not see the snow drifts, the sleet, the grinding towers of ice that subsequently descended on the town.

As Bob Dylan once croaked, the times they are a-changin', but all he had to worry about was the invention of the yoyo and flared pants, not global warming and impending ice ages. Science tells us that the increased planetary temperature is caused by Justin Timberlake and cow flatulence (which are really the same thing), combined with McDonald's wrappers and middle-class apathy wrought by years of moral decay. Or something. Maybe it's just Justin Timberlake.

Whatever it is, the northern hemisphere has been sizzling while Ceres residents fire up their snowcats to rescue icebound postmen at the bottom of the driveway. And if climate change is here to stay, perhaps it's time to start preparing for a radically altered world.

In 2025 our globe is a very different place, except for Cliff Richard who still looks 60 despite being 135, and naturally sport has adapted. Every year motor-sport enthusiasts flock to the Cairo–Berlin rally, where buggies and bikes leave the temperate woodland of North Africa to take on the dunes of Provence, pushing on up the Rhine Canyon, fighting their way through the baking quicksand-infested plains of the Netherlands (watched by nomadic bands of Belgians offering beads and chocolates in return for water and trinkets) and finally passing under the exotic minarets and shaded markets of the German capital's Hauptstrasse.

To the north, in the rainforests of Finland, leathery rally drivers nudge their machines through steaming mud and through sluggish rivers choked with creepers and Ukrainian shrimp-fishermen, while away to the east in Mongolia, mild summer afternoons pass to the gentle crack of leather on willow as the Ulan Bator XI bats out a good-natured draw against the Genghis Khan Wanderers.

The southern hemisphere has embraced new sporting opportunities. South Africa rules the rugby roost by default: most of New Zealand and Australia are submerged, and England and France can no longer afford the luxury of making leather balls for sport, using them instead for carrying rainwater and for chewing on when camel-meat is in short supply. Not surprisingly the charm of the game has waned, and South Africans have found new pastimes. Escarpment-skiing is extremely popular, a marvellous two-day event that requires little or no effort as the competitor launches from a standing start in Johannesburg and slowly gathers speed through the Free State and Karoo until he or she plunges into a huge puddle in Cape Town, dehydrated, snow-blind, and madly exhilarated.

Likewise the Durban-to-Pietermaritzburg swim draws thousands of competitors every summer, and television audiences watch enthralled as the last dregs thrash towards the finish line, desperate to reach the Maritzburg docks before the final gun is fired and the shark nets are raised …

Of course there will always be pole-vaulting and sprinting, even if the pole-vaulter lands in a snowdrift and the sprinters need Factor 30 sun block for those 9.2 seconds in the sun, but for the rest it will be a case of adapt or die. And at the rate the Springboks adapted out of Ceres, it looks like we've already got a head start.

The Guru

People thought I made this up. At least those who had heard of Deepak thought so. Others just thought a Deepak was one of those beanbags you stick in the microwave when you've got a stiff neck. And in many ways he is.

By harnessing the power of the platitude, guru-for-hire Deepak Chopra has lightened the wallets of bored housewives for over a decade, but a charlatan he is not. Indeed, his admirers fervently believe that he possesses supernatural sensitivities, and this seems beyond dispute: along with being able to put a lively audience into a deep sleep in less than ten minutes, he can smell money at a thousand yards and can distinguish between American Express and Visa even with a nose-cold.

Furthermore, using mind-over-matter techniques of deep relaxation and transcendental denial he has convinced the West that India is a lotus-carpeted nirvana lousy with enlightenment and oozing tranquillity, rather than a 50-year-old motorbike carrying a billion people, a cow and some suitcases during rush hour.

Perhaps the matrons of Montana and Michigan are wising up, or maybe Deepak has simply run out of mystical ways to describe brushing teeth and making toast. Whatever the case, there's a smell of desperation about his latest book – it seems a guru shall not live by caviar alone – and the only aura around *Golf for Enlightenment* is the glint of a rented tanning-bed off a Rolex.

Golf coaches do talk an awful lot of rot. I was once told by a ferociously hairy homunculus on a swampy North Carolina fairway to 'pitcher yer swangin' yer clurb at a terrapin'. It was never made clear why one would want to bludgeon a turtle with a 9-iron, but that was his schtick and it worked for him. However, even the most glib pro would draw the line at advice like 'Find the now and you'll find the shot', a chapter that explains in 15 000 words how to keep your head over the ball and swing through the line.

At this rate golf tournaments could last months as players glide off into the woods to find the now, or desperately jet off to Bhutan to consult their swamis when the now has become now and then, and is threatening to become entirely then. Technicalities would be nightmarish: can caddies be dispatched to find the now? Is a penalty enforced if the now is found out of bounds? Oy vay.

However, if the now has been misplaced somewhere, one can simply ask the ball for directions, for according to another interminable chapter, 'The ball knows everything'. Hegelian philosophy, the lyrics to *The Phantom of the Opera*, how to make a delicious flan – those inscrutable little Pings have known all of it all along. Suspicious minds might wonder why balls can't get themselves out of water hazards more frequently, perhaps fashioning a rudimentary pulley with water-weeds and hubcaps, but Deepak does not go so far as to suggest that they have opposable thumbs, so there they stay, brooding and omniscient down in the muck.

It all has something to do with the Tree of Knowledge, which caused Adam and Eve to become the world's first squatters. The chapter entitled 'Playing in the Garden of Eden' disappointingly does not endorse nude co-ed golfing

41

romps but instead bangs on about the philosophy of gardening. It seems that golf courses are our sad attempts to recreate Eden, which apparently had lots of bunkers all over it (tended by archangels with flaming rakes), and a sprinkler system that came on at five every morning.

If balls represent the apple, then the serpent is surely the furtive biped who emerges sodden from reeds and canals and drains along one's way, clutching five muddy chipped orbs (either balls or crocodile eggs, one can't tell) that can be yours for just R5 each. With three of your original five balls already deep in meditation at the bottom of ponds, and six holes remaining, the offer is sweet, tempting; but the sign at the clubhouse promises immediate expulsion to anyone caught partaking of these soggy bargains …

Deepak might have got away with it, splashing his insipid watercolour prose about with enough generalisations to escape being busted; but it all comes to a crashing halt with a little subheading tucked away between the Zen and the now: You Can Master This Game.

Sure, *we* can master this game, but can Deepak? His absence from the PGA top earners' list suggests that you don't have to wear a string vest and a ratty John Deere baseball cap to be an ignorant yokel yelling advice at the pros from the sidelines.

Love fifteen, and bring
them along to watch

I'm just bitter because my tennis career – that unhappy summer of 1996 – was witnessed only by a school combi and a flyblown bottle of lukewarm Oros.

Right now, somewhere in the world, three events are taking place. Somewhere, a teenager is dying a slow excruciating death as 'Happy Birthday' is bellowed at him by pimply steak-ranch waiters. Meanwhile across the globe, in a tinsel-festooned Bangkok karaoke bar, a Japanese tourist is listening to a Korean businessman sing the Beatles' 'Yesterday': Yesseraaay ore my trabor seem saw fa awaaay …

According to the statisticians who work out these things, those two songs are performed all day every day: indeed, Spur waiters alone account for around 80 per cent of the former's performances. But the bean-counters have missed the third eternal event, because somewhere, right now, someone in dark glasses is nervously chewing on a programme in the support-ers' box at a tennis tournament.

Research done by NASA and the National Geographic Society reveals that the most plentiful things in the world are (in order) bits of sand, locusts, professional tennis tourna-ments, lemmings, dormice and Baldwins. It is probably not an exaggeration to suggest that all the world's tennis courts cover an area equivalent to Switzerland. (Alas, nobody has thought of improving Switzerland by levelling it, covering it in green concrete and painting white lines all over it ... yet.) And where the ATP tour goes, there go the Significant Others.

The box reserved for kin and loved ones is a curious zoo, combining aristocratic poise with Russian Mafia taste. The parents, when on speaking terms or not in prison, invariably sit at the front, leathery and hawkish, their rumps moulded by a billion bucket seats and their osteoporosis-ravaged wrists splintering under the weight of bejewelled Rolexes. The coach, a ferocious Greek person with a crazed Afro bobbing in the breeze, glowers over what is either a moustache or a Shetland pony glued to his lip. He passes the time nervously plaiting the hair on his forearms.

But Mumsy and Pater, bushy Stavros, all of them pale into insignificance next to The Current Partners. Blushing dew-drops with bouffant hair and false lashes, they sit and agonise for their hero down on the court, glued-on nails ground up between miracles of dentistry. All the greats brought these perfumed meringues to watch them at work: Pete Sampras, Martina Navratilova ...

And speaking of Pistol Pete, when he finally retires and starts making a living winning Hansie Cronje look-alike competitions, some of the glorious chintz will disappear from the game for good. Until the late 1990s, when athletic blondes became the necessary accessory, he could be relied upon every year to bring along some new vision in puce, a Liberace dream of shoulder-pads and lavender rouge, the daughter of the Katzenjammers of Long Island and three-time winner of the West Egg Ladies' Quilt-a-thon. The lovelies came and went like Pete's hairline, but soon it will all be over.

Steffi Graf does clean up very nicely, but watching her root for André Agassi one gets the feeling she knows too much: vhy, she seems to be wondering, does der stupit Amerikaner homunculus not drill it up der tremlines instead of zis cross-court forehand foolishness? Somehow it spoils the illusion of trusting admiration so carefully nurtured by heiresses throughout the 1980s. No, tennis partners should never think about anything more than the next Saturday's rowing regatta and whether the Bolly in the limo was put on ice early enough.

One must hasten to add that in our egalitarian times the Significant Other up in the box does not have to be female by any manner of means. The current crop of Belgian waffles winning tournaments, 16-year-old matrons with surnames like Clijsters's and Henin, all install their beaux in the family booth. Apart from Lleyton Hewitt, whose outbursts of Aussie joy at Kim Clijsters's successes cause him to beat unconscious anyone near him and then fart a reasonable facsimile of 'Waltzing Matilda', these lads are as polished and nebulous as any Samprasian conquest. One would never suspect that behind the perfect hair and the dimples there lurk professional skateboarders called Chad or experimental tag-artists called Mario-X.

The Agassi-Grafs aside, these liaisons rarely last. The tour moves on, and so do its stars. In suddenly empty Park Avenue apartments shoulder-pads and dark glasses are packed away, stuffed fuzzy tennis racquets tearfully burned, and life becomes dull and meaningless. At least for the afternoon. Because this evening there's bridge, and then that marvellous new show called *Crud*, by Mario-X ...

If you go down to the
woods today ...

A friend with family in the frozen north told me he'd sent this to his Newfy kin. I haven't heard from him since. I hope the local Labrador sheriff has opened a docket and ordered his sergeant to wake up the dogs and rub some linseed oil into them snowshoes, eh.

Canadians are a restrained lot. When they get angry, they go to a symphony and stew in the cheap seats. When they get really angry, for instance when they encounter racial intolerance or impure maple syrup, they go to a symphony but decline to buy a programme. Old-timers in Quebec still talk about one infamous sociopath who blew his nose during a Beethoven slow movement; but revisionist historians are insisting the man was the victim of allergies and are campaigning to have his descendants rehabilitated and repatriated to Canada.

Michael Moore's *Bowling for Columbine* made much of Canadians' unearthly ability to refrain from blowing each other away en masse. Indeed Moore is not alone in punting Canucks as a race wedged firmly between Swedes and Seraphim, a Norman Rockwell painting with polar bears instead of beagles, where rapping is something Daryl and Doris do on the front door when they come over with pecan pie and Pat Boone records.

But morality is being confused with practicality. It's not

that Canadians aren't trying to waste each other, it's just fairly difficult to engage in effective gun-play when one's aim is obscured by clouds of condor-sized mosquitoes; and what with all those pesky noise regulations you have to wrap your equaliser in a towel, and there's nothing worse than a perforated bath-towel, so what's the point?

With all this pent-up rage about, it comes as no surprise that rubbing one's corduroy trouser-legs together loudly at the Philharmonic doesn't always cut it. Sometimes Canadian men snap. After a long day in the local Greenpeace office, all they want to do is have a quiet tofu snack with their Life Partner, have a long talk about the relationship with him/her/it, before turning in on the futon and drifting off to a CD of Navajo chants. But noooo, he/she/it doesn't want to talk tonight, he/she/it has a headache. There are accusations of acting out, counter-accusations of sublimation and passive aggression. The word 'hermaphrodite' inevitably crops up, and that's when men go to the woods to play sport.

North American sports broadcasters have given these woodland frolics frenzied names involving grizzly bears and lumberjacks, but it's tough to make high-speed split-second-timed bark-stripping sound like anything other than what addled beavers get up to. Still, it is nice to know that should the ESPN2 John Deere Bug-B-Gone Extreme Woodsman of 2003 ever get trapped out in the tundra, he will be able to build a double-storey log cabin with escalator, conservatory and ballroom in under four minutes with nothing but a hacksaw and two bungees.

The chainsaw events draw the biggest crowds since there's always that tiny chance of seeing someone saw off their coach's head should the grizzled old bloke lean in too close. But there's plenty to choose from for the thousands of hardy souls who come to watch, babies and puppies strapped to their bodies to prevent them being carried off into the mountains by the mosquitoes. If chainsaw sculpture is not your bag, there's manual sawing, redwood-climbing, sawdust-chewing, everything one could ever want from a day spent in gumboots in an Arctic swamp full of mulch and the desiccated carcasses of elk sucked dry.

Sometimes, just sometimes, one feels that all is not well in the mind of the Extreme Woodsman. Yes, he never broke a sweat as he carved Rodin's 'The Kiss' out of a ten-foot slab of teak, but consider the axe challenge. It is no coincidence that Jack Nicholson was wearing a checked shirt, lumberjack jacket and work boots when he took a chopper to the bathroom door in *The Shining:* when the chips are flying and the axe whooshing about, a nasty gleam appears in the eye of our woodsman, and one can only imagine the fantasies of Canadian carnage that he indulges for a wild few minutes: hacking up that ergonomically designed chair his Life Partner makes him sit in at dinner, cleaving tonight's microscopic portion of sushi before going to the drive-through burger joint, stalking the nine Maltese poodles in the Animal Rescue Haven outside his bedroom window …

After that, why would you want to shoot anyone?

Dismal decimals

Recently someone who'd only ever seen me in my by-line photo told me that I was lot bigger than he'd expected. I can only assume he'd measured my face and extrapolated from there, putting me at some-where around 8 centimetres in my socks, or in the old language, $3\frac{1}{3}$ inches.

My generation knows plenty, despite being born after the death of Elvis. We know, for instance, that in 1972 a crack commando unit was sent to prison for a crime they didn't commit, and that these men promptly escaped to the Los Angeles underground, where they now survive as soldiers of fortune. We know that if you have a problem, and if no one else can help, and if you can find them, maybe you can hire … the A-Team.

Suckled on lip-synching, we are karaoke savants. We know that Kylie Minogue (before her orthodontic renaissance) once wondered why she was so lucky and that Belinda Carlisle wanted a light left on for her. Like singers of ancient lays, we chant in unison the dialogue of *Dirty Dancing*. Ferris Bueller is our spiritual mentor, and Thomas Magnum lives in the basement of our subconscious, surrounded by rubber chickens.

But venture back into the primeval mists of the mid-1970s, plunge into the Neolithic sludge of the 1960s and the Precambrian swamps of the 1950s, and we become less certain of things. And nothing is more confounding to us than the notion that once, impossibly long ago, people used something other than the decimal system.

It seems that before decimalisation South Africa's currency used to work as follows: there were seventeen pence to a farthing, and fourteen and a half farthings (or twelve, depending on the angle of the sun) to a florin. A florin was worth nine million pounds, which was equivalent to six and a third cowry shells or three British Protectorates, not including Bechuanaland. Cash registers looked like church organs.

With the arrival of the decimal comma, accountancy became a profession instead of a vocation, and tickies stopped being worth one-seven-millionth of a cowry shell and started lurking in Christmas pudding, grinding molars to dust. And the apparatchiks of the new system rooted out every reference to the old measurements with a zeal that would have been Inquisitorial had it not been so thoroughly modern.

Not even the Bible was spared: after decimalisation Genesis (or, in the Decimal Gospel, Book 1.0, module 6.160000) revealed how The Great Decimilator instructed His servant Noah to make 'the length of the ark 135 metres, its breadth 22.5 metres, and its height 13.5 metres … For behold, I will bring a flood of waters upon the earth, to kill 100.0001 per cent (better safe than sorry) of all flesh, in which is the breath of life, from under heaven …'

Even today the long shadow of that accursed comma lies across the landscape. Last week a piece in this newspaper about Pakistani fast bowler Shoaib Akhtar ended up commatose after a cardinal in the Inquisition of Editorial Correctitude painstakingly changed every reference to miles per hour to kilometres per hour. Poor Shoaib ended up robbed, having to settle for an anaemic 161 kph instead of the Holy Grail of 100 mph.

But it is reassuring that even in a devoutly decimal country such as ours, sport refuses to toe the decimal line. England is still likely to win the rugby World Cup by a country mile rather than a pastoral 1,6093 km span. Likewise Shaun Pollock would seem an entirely less formidable customer should he exchange his line six inches outside off stump for one 15,24 cm away (although it would be nice to see him regain the 0,9144 m of pace he's lost over the years). And it's no wonder the West Indies can't produce great fast bowlers any more: they're all 2,01 metres tall these days, not a six-foot-eight monster among the lot of them.

The fact that the Proclaimers were willing to walk 500 miles (and then 500 more) pales into insignificance when one remembers that Roger Bannister galloped the length of one in under four minutes. But Sir Roger's breathless dash and its reeling finish is robbed of all its pioneering greatness by those who wish us to remember that he took 3,975 minutes to run just over 1,6 kilometres.

Boxing promoters might get excited about junior feather-weight boxers tipping the scales at 42,6384 kg, but they're still 94-pound weaklings to the rest of us. That is until they turn into 300-pound behemoths and decide to sit on everyone who called them Stringbean, at which point the difference between 136,08 kg and 136,09 kg is useful only to judge the exact length of time one will spend in traction.

All of which is a roundabout way of saying: you stick in a comma, you lose the point.

The King and I:
The missing Diana letters

The secret letters of the late Princess of Wales were revealed to a palpitating Britain, each a paragon of kitsch and sentimentality to be lapped up by the sort of people who move their lips when reading. But South Africans were already moving their lips: we had streamed out in our dozens to buy the tell-all autobiography of Louis Luyt; and I couldn't help wondering what the result might have been had the Candle in the Wind ever indulged in a secret correspondence with our Spanner in the Works.

Dear Mr Luyt, thank you so much for the signed World Cup rugby ball. It took me some time to realise that all 120 autographs on it were yours, but Charles and I think it a charming addition to our gift vault, and have mounted it next to our shrunken human head. Next time you are in London please do come to the palace gift shop and sign the visitors' book. Yours sincerely, Diana, Princess of ~~Whales~~ ~~Wails~~ Wales. (Sorry … those bloody Welsh and their spelling!)

Dear Prinses, please don't be so formal: my closest friends call me Meneer or Baas, and I would be honoured if you would do the same. Please accept another small token of my esteem. Yours, Oswald Louis Petrus Poleÿ Luyt.

Dear Baas Luyt, thank you so much for your gift of your old rugby socks. Their bouquet is rustic yet cheeky, reminiscent, one feels, of a damp Labrador some weeks dead. Thank you also for enclosing the draft manuscript of your autobiography: my Afrikaans is not what it should be, but the picture on the front looks jolly fascinating. Yours, etcetera.

Dear Prinses, at the risk of sounding gushy, you are not half bad considering you are a Rooinek agitator and a woman and you live in a country that is a festering pustule oozing with homosexuality, Satanism, rock music and Elton John. Manchester is quite nice, though. The rest is crap.

Dear Baas, I am so enjoying reading *Hensoppers, Communists, Traitors: The Judas Pienaar and His Place in the Global ANC Rugby Conspiracy.* I have never read such a long book before: tomorrow night I shall reach page 80, and then rest for a few days and admire the wonderful pictures. Which reminds me: the Quartermaster-General of the Royal Marines has asked me to ask you what your diet is, since he thinks it could feed an army. Any secret tips? Personally, I find wheat-free breadsticks and dairy-free yoghurt do very nicely when one needs comfort food. XX HRH Di.

Dear Prinses, usually I start my day with a breakfast of quail tongues and deep-fried moose-haunch, but bloody Riaan Oberholzer has hung a big picture of Mandela and the Judas holding up my World Cup on the dining-room wall and now I can't get any food down. Soentjies, LL.

Dear Baas, I think you are being far too sensitive. Will Carling once told me that Mr Pienaar looked splendid in his underpants (I still don't know what he was doing in Will's underpants), and as for Mr Mandela, when I met him he was a complete gentleman. He told me all about his childhood in the West Indies, and how difficult it was getting a lead role in Hollywood in the 1960s. Funny, he kept telling me that his name was Sidney Poitier. Do you suppose that was his tribal name? I know he's a Maori or a Zulu or a Mormon or something, and they do have queer names!

Dear Prinses, I think our relationship has progressed to a point where I wouldn't mind if you wanted to address me as Field Marshal or Your Honour. Meanwhile, dinners have become impossible: Riaan sits there staring at me with those baleful little blue eyes of his, shooting rubber bands at me and chanting 'I'm the boss of the SARFU and you're not!' And no one wants to vote for my political party, despite my stylist saying I have the chins of Marlon Brando and the hair of Napoleon. What should I do? My chef suggests food poisoning, but no one organises decent fatal poisonings any more. Help! LL

Dear Baas Field Marshal, when I get cross I donate money to the clearing of landmines. They're so clever these days: if it were up to me, I'd drop bags of £1 coins out of a zeppelin and see if any mines went off, but Prince Philip says that's a stupid idea, like giving Africa independence. Prince Philip fell asleep in a scone the other morning, looked pretty terminal. The London stock exchange surged 100 points at the news, but the Queen woke him up with a kipper down his shirt. Don't know why I mentioned it … damn this new hair-spray, it makes me all woozy.

Dear Prinses … getting dark … afraid … Riaan's beady eyes … rubber bands … hensoppers … Judas starring in Lays ads on TV, can't look but can't look away … government taking over rugby … planting chips in brains … Lays … die kreun van ossewa … urgh.

Guys and Dollars

Damon Runyon, the guy who is writing 'Guys and Dolls' some years back, is a favourite of mine. In fact any guy who has not yet read classics like 'Butch Minds the Baby' or 'The Hottest Guy in the World' and has not met characters like Izzy Cheesecake (who is called Izzy Cheesecake because all the time he is eating cheesecake) is missing out more than somewhat. Also if he is not reading much of Runyon the odds is good that this piece about early World Cup Bid spooning will go down like a pork sausage at a bar mitzvah.

So I am minding my own business last week when who should walk into the diner but two parties by the name of Dapper Danny Jordaan and Knuckles Balfour, and both are looking more than somewhat blue. It also seems that Dapper Danny hasn't slept in days, and his suit is hanging off him like newsprint off a bum, but then this is not unusual for Dapper Danny so I let it slide.

Knuckles orders half a pound of bacon, and they get to talking. It seems there's this dame, goes by the name of Fifa. Yeah, I say, I hear of her. Everybody knows Fifa. I don't mention that Fifa is a mighty lame name for a gal because Dapper Danny is mooning around like he's going to blub any moment.

So it seems Fifa is in town, just passing through on her way home to Europe. Larry Lips tells me last week that she runs a sweatshop that makes soccer balls, and that her accounting system has more holes in it than Stinky Freddy Fishfingers the night he tries to whack Twitchy Alfredo down at the pier and forgets to load his equaliser, but this is another story. And besides, I can see that Dapper Danny and Knuckles Balfour (now just ordering another half-pound of bacon) are what you call smitten, and have clearly been pitching woo at the dame in question, so I say nothing.

It turns out both parties are trying to persuade the doll to come for a longer visit in 2010, but she is being coy and whispering sweet nothings to both and generally teasing them. Why, I say, this sounds like a job for Big Nelson.

Now back in the day Big Nelson does 27 years in the slammer for tossing pineapples at railroads and suchlike, and after he gets out he goes into small-time politics and writes a whole book by himself, called *The Long Crawl to Freedom* or something along those lines, about escaping from the cooler. I do not read this book after I hear it features no gunplay and less burlesque, but he does not drop any in my estimation for not being able to write a realistic story.

Big Nelson is on the wrong side of 80, but he is still a ladykiller despite the long crawl, and if there is one guy who can romance a dame like Fifa, it is he. Not a day goes by that Big Nelson does not have some doll on his arm, even if sometimes that doll is a very sturdy nurse who seems to be giving him a little push now and then. And Missis Big Nelson, Gracy Machel Ma Belle, always looks as happy as the widow Finkelstein after old man Finkelstein the millionaire accidentally beat himself to death with a candelabra.

These fellows is made men in their own right, and not eager to admit in public that they can't romance a dame like Fifa. And besides (and this is between you and me) I hear it said that Fifa is not the toughest date in town: without meaning to impugn what is left of her reputation, she is the kind of gal who will be your ever-loving wife and your mother-in-law for enough folding money, and word is that Dapper Dan and Knuckles have leaned on a couple of banks and raised enough green to make the scene. Don't get me wrong about Fifa: nothing she could do could make me think less of her. She is just not my kind of doll.

I hear it goes swell, with Fifa fluttering eyelashes and lashing on the rouge in one corner of a booth at Lindy's, and Big Nelson ever the gent in the other corner. Dapper Danny and Knuckles try and squeeze in on either side of Big Nelson, but Knuckles has been putting away the gefilte fish and it is something of a tight fight, so they take the booth next door, and play craps and try and listen to what is being said until finally Big Nelson give Fifa a big peck on the cheek and they call a cab, and hightail it uptown.

'He is a swell guy,' says Dapper Danny, 'but I think he has stole our gal.'

'Mm,' says Knuckles, working at a crème brûlée like a safebreaker with a rubber drill.

Later, I ask Big Nelson what goes on uptown, but he says a gentleman never tells.

I have a dream ...

In which the Snobby Green Bank messes with the wrong financially embarrassed columnist.

Those who can, do. Those who can't, teach. If Woody Allen is to be believed, those who can't teach, teach gym. And those who can't teach gym, write advertisements for radio. Typing troglodytes, bottom-feeders infatuated with word-processors, these vendors of numbing banality cling to the sphincter of human discourse, hawking verbless exhortations to action and the battered corpses of 60-year-old puns. In their hands thirty seconds is an eternity.

So when the reassuring drawl of Gary Player rose clear above the aural sludge, I sat up and listened. Gary was urging me to open an account with Nedbank, which was dashed altruistic of him considering he doesn't even work for them. If I opened an account, Gary told me, Nedbank – out of the goodness of its great big freshly-baked sun-dappled dew-sprinkled heart – would give one needy child a ...

Long-overdue thrashing? No, banks only brutalise people with an income. So what bounty was Nedbank about to scatter to the throng of ululating cherubim? Would the opening of my account give a needy child a meal a day? A classroom with a roof? Gary's voice supported a tone of exquisitely noble suffering, while outside my window a team of municipal labourers broke into a chorus of 'When you wish upon a star'.

Staggered by my innate goodness, I lunged for the telephone, eager to dedicate my life to Nedbank so that the little children might live. But true rapture was still to come: Gary finished his sentence. Open an account, he revealed, and Nedbank will give one needy child a pair of golf shoes.

Thank God for Nedbank and Gary Player and their immaculate timing. Just last year the United Nations stopped delivering truckloads of golf shoes to the developing world. In Myanmar, North Korea and Liberia there are an estimated 150 pairs of golf shoes, 120 of them with at least one cleat missing. A 2002 report by Médecins Sans Frontières featured the chilling estimate that, if sanctions were not lifted against Iraq, children would have no choice but to stop playing golf altogether. And in Afghanistan, where handicaps are decreed under Sharia law, the Kabul Country Club is now used to grow poppies for the banquet halls of St Andrews, a stark testament to the West's cynical abandonment of Afghan golf.

Without wanting to exaggerate my virtue, I did once try to give a needy child a pair of golf shoes. That is, I once tried to open an account at Nedbank. A limp and patronising creature with prehensile jowls held my bank statement like a soiled nappy, and informed me that there was a minimum balance required, and I had best try elsewhere, 'somewhere without entry standards'. As I left he took out a can of air freshener and cleansed his cubicle before straightening his toupee and continuing work on his rubber-band ball.

Now surely this was a case for targeted charity? If my account couldn't have afforded a pair of shoes, how about some balls? Or those overpriced tiddlywinks discs one bangs down on the green whenever one wants to blow one's nose or look thoughtful? This Christmas little Shadrack will sit in his family's shack, writing a letter to Santa by the light of a guttering candle:

'Dear Santa, since grandma died on the back nine at Fancourt it has been very difficult for us. Dad drowned in the water hazard at Royal Cape last year, and Mom ran away with a caddie at Augusta, and grandma's pension used to cover our membership fees, but now we can only manage one round a month. Please Santa, I have four irons, a putter and a driver, but I had to sell my divot fixer to pay for Thandi's lunch yesterday. Could you bring me a new one?'

Once, Shadrack would have been denied, forced to sell his 6-iron for school fees. But today he has Nedbank, Gary Player and God on his side.

The last paraphrase should go to Martin Luther King: 'I have a dream that one day on the green fairways of Georgia the sons of former slaves and the sons of former slaveowners will be able to tee off together in a four-ball of brotherhood … I have a dream that my four children will one day live in a nation where they will not be judged by the colour of their skin but by the contents of their golf bags. I have a dream today.' Amen, brother.

What's in a name?

According to an account I received last year, my name is Eton Mr Thomas 7708 Tom. Perhaps in time I shall change my name by deed poll to 7708, which manages effortlessly to convey the glamour of a life in British espionage while expressing a deep respect for cultural roots, in this case represented by a Cape Town postal code.

How fortunate to raise one's children in a trailer park, free of the terrible responsibility of having to match a name to an infant. How marvellous to be able to summon one's offspring with a brisk ping on the nearest hubcap, or with a belch, or, in moments of tenderness, by yelling 'C'mere, you!'

The rest of us must pore over tomes of names, fretting about matching meanings with one-week-old personalities. Will little Lucius, now setting fire to his cot with Dad's Zippo, be a shining light in the world? Will little Felix, howling for seven hours without taking a breath, be happy?

Many parents, it seems, have abandoned the search for a name that signifies sweetness and light. Take poor Chad, for example, a youth apparently named after a flyblown killing-field west of Libya and two inches short of hell. Little Izan's parents don't seem to care that their precious baby girl is a backward Nazi. Indeed, our tykes galloping about the trailer park have dodged a bullet by going unnamed: who knows what monstrosities of nomenclature might have been grafted to their little souls? Chevron-Duane … Bethani-Shayne … JayLo-Oprah-Botox …

If we can't name each other with some sort of dignity and intelligence, what chance do we have of labelling our sports teams coherently? For all their sins, Rudolf the Red-Faced and Riaan Oberholzer (whose name, peculiarly enough, means either 'Little King' or 'Maiden' or 'Mud', depending on who you ask) never tried to sex up the name of the national rugby team. Silas (or 'Forest') Nkanunu, clearly unable to see the wood for the trees, still restrained himself from dubbing them the Nike Castle Supa-Phly Rugga Boyz.

The same cannot be said for other teams. Northerns rugby player and twinkle-toed monolith Geo Cronje has had a rough few months, but nothing could quite match the indignity of having to introduce himself at dinner parties as a Mobil Blou Bul. Still, rather that than playing for the Telkom Callmore Mighty Elephants, a name that conjures endless delays, five-ton repair-men crushing switchboards under their flat feet while their noses probe delicately for loose wires and marula fruit.

Cricket too has lost it entirely. Once it was enough to refer to 'the Gentlemen's XI' or, at a gauche pinch, 'England'. Today the Sussex Sharks proudly fly the flag of inanity, since the only sharks near Hove are either chopped into tiny freeze-dried cubes and hidden in the holds of passing Taiwanese trawlers, or sitting in the boardrooms of county executive committees. At least the Warwickshire Bears can claim to be harking back to some Medieval Olde England Utopia. Certainly they have it better than the Nottinghamshire Witch-Burners and the Middlesex Plague-Sores.

Of course it is soccer, often the sanctuary of the criminally insane and irrevocably dull, that sets the tone when it comes to names. Bafana Bafana have somehow got away with their title, although it remains to be seen when the boys the boys will grow into the men the men. Given the sleepy, backwoodsy style of South African football, perhaps it is time they were renamed Mañana Mañana. And it seemed that only a mind far gone on malt liquor and penalty shootouts could have named our national Under-5 (or something) soccer team the Tsetse Flies, but there was clearly method in this madness: what better moniker for a team that buzzes about in random circles before putting its victims into a deep and fatal sleep?

But we're still babes in the Silas compared with this week's fiasco in the little Californian town of Irvine. Local Muslim youngsters organised a Muslim Football tournament (which, just to clarify, has the same rules as Secular Football). All good clean fun, athletic lads stretching their legs in the West Coast sunshine. Until three teams decided to call themselves Mujaheddin, Intifada, and Soldiers of Allah …

One can only imagine the suicide tackles, all three teams simultaneously claiming responsibility via pre-recorded videos for spraining their opponent's ankle, the mass demonstrations at the sending off of the guilty culprit, the red-carded fellow blaming American colonialism for forcing him to go in with the boot.

Perhaps in next year's tournament, hosted by the Guantánamo Maximum Security Sports Facility, they can take a leaf from South Africa's name book. Osama Osama has rather a nice ring to it.

Lost and found

Way back in December 2003 when this appeared, the Americans were still looking for Weapons of Mass Destruction but so far had found only a tousled Persian rug hiding in a hole. Meanwhile South Africa's selectors were still looking for a spin bowler but so far had found only Robin Peterson and a still-smoking cricket ball wedged in a billboard half a mile down the road from the Wanderers.

Critics of American tactics in Iraq said that searching for Saddam Hussein was like looking for a needle in a haystack. As it turned out, it was like looking for a fat man in a long-drop. Saddam, fiend and hellraiser that he is, has been whiling away his autumn years plaiting his beard while reading the Geneva Convention for the first time.

His burrow was lined with $750 000 in cash, but it is certain he went in with a million or two: a bloke's got to blow his nose on something. He always vowed he wouldn't be taken alive, and a pistol and two AKs suggested that a martyring had been on the cards; but somehow those little bullets just looked so darned sharp ... Not that a bullet would have been able to penetrate that filthy coif anyway: he could have made a break for freedom, American rounds ricocheting off his crusty 'fro as he scampered towards the Syrian border.

His capture is the stuff of which memoirs are made: *I Shaved Saddam: A Barber Remembers; You Filthy Swab: My Part in Brushing Hussein's Teeth on National Television*. The cooking of Saddam's goose is also the best Christmas present the news media could have wished for. In the United States the broadsheets in the coming days will be crammed with memory-refreshing pop quizzes: 'We hate this guy because: (a) he bombed Pearl Harbour; (b) he tried to shoot down Tom Cruise in *Top Gun*; (c) he boycotted the 1999 Oscars; d) all of the above.' *The Guardian* will denounce the violation of a prisoner's right to a private interrogation, under a full-page colour photo of Saddam's tonsils; while in a sizzling editorial *The Times* of Syria will reveal that the Americans were inflicting imperialist dental hygiene on a Hollywood-bred Zionist body-double and then demand more Western aid for Syrian toothbrush factories which can no longer afford top-notch depleted uranium.

Even now *Huisgenoot* is putting together a picture special on the great dictator's hideout, 'Pragfoto's van Saddam se gat'.

With so much publicity it won't be long before estate agents are arriving in Tikrit, their floral jumpsuits covered in camel spit and their gold-rimmed specs encrusted with flies. Saddam's last stand will sell for plenty. La Grotto, a renovator's dream! Snug and private, ideal for the single guy who likes to let it all hang out. Do-it-yourself plumbing, plus built-in floor-size Zen garden with free sand!

The ideal bachelor pad, for instance, for cricketer Robin Peterson. Termed a spin bowler because of his ability to spin round to watch the ball he has just delivered soar over the pavilion roof, Peterson was looking for a hole in the ground at the Wanderers at the weekend. A month of solitude, with R50 in cash and two *Beano* annuals, could be just the thing to soothe away those Brian Lara blues.

But Robin would have to fight off Rudolf Straeuli, also

dead keen to get his mitts on some Iraqi real estate. Not to hide in – fired incompetent South African coaches are genetically unable to experience embarrassment – but as a future asset to SARFU when he is welcomed back into the fold as a coaching assistant.

Already the Straeuli dining-room table is covered with charts and blueprints outlining his second coming. The manuscript of his memoirs, *Mein Kamps*, props up a blonde voodoo doll wearing an England number 10 jersey. Let us peruse a page …

'… made entirely out of rubber, and flexible beyond my wildest dreams. But I digress. Have been studying hamsters lately. Beautiful creatures. Wild and free. Have begun to understand the folly of trying to out-muscle a foe: size is irrelevant when one has expandable cheeks and the ability to sleep for nine months of the year. This is the future. Tiny rugby players, ferocious, omnivorous, narcoleptic. The world will stand back in awe, and everyone will say sorry and stop talking about my cauliflower ears. Thoughts on Staaldraad 2: how to find a dwarf backline? Will make them carry boxes of Quality Street until they vomit. Crucial to success of plan: 35 hours in Tikrit hole in ground – perhaps spray them with honey and insert bees? Excellent for team spirit, also looks kind of hot. God I miss my army days …'

History in the maiming

Everything you think is new, says John Cusack in 'City Hall', is just the history you don't know.

There's nothing like a big shiny trophy to give closet nationalists the sporting hots. The same shabby politicos who spent their days at Patrice Lumumba University struggling through the all-in-pictures version of *Das Kapital* and decrying sport as the pastime of the bourgeoisie now embrace victories as proof of their nation's manifest destiny and their God-given duty to extend their term of office by a decade or thereabouts.

The Springboks' mercifully early exit from the Rugby World Cup last year [2003] no doubt thwarted the hastily-dusted-off anthropologists who were being lined up to tell us the Africanist truth about the sport; of its origins as a Nubian fertility ritual, how the rugby traditions of ancient Sudan were lost over time as none of their neighbours wanted to play with them, the Yoruba to the south being too busy inventing cricket while the Pharaohs of the Nile were booked solid with golfing engagements.

It is disappointing that Thabo Mbeki's court historian failed to unearth the origins of baseball during the President's touch-and-go visit of that blighted armpit of Caribbean squalor, Haiti: on an island that combines an exotic blend of imported voodoo and organically grown racist violence with an inexhaustible enthusiasm for hitting things with clubs, it seems certain that priestesses drenched in chicken blood have been slugging shrunken human heads into the bleachers for generations. Indeed in 1915, when one of Haiti's rulers was chopped into tiny pieces by his constituents and carried through the streets, the most sought-after presidential cutlet must have been the head, with the new generalissimo eagerly awaiting the inaugural pitch at the Port-au-Prince Stadium.

But perhaps one is being too harsh. It was, after all, colonisation – only 112 years in the past by 1915 – that forced the oppressed masses to turn their president into sirloin, and as usual one needs to point the finger north to Europe and England. England, the first evil empire (apart from the Philistines, the Aztecs, the Assyrians, the Romans, the Mongols and the Dutch) and the people responsible for plague, Hitler, firebombing, Elton John, human sacrifice, Merchant-Ivory films and Saudi Arabia. Surely those pasty expansionists have an immense revisionist mythology built around their national sports by now, three centuries after stealing them from Africa?

That would certainly be the case if Britons knew any history. David versus Goliath? Weren't that when Becks took on Arsenal all by himself? Yer, 3-1, innit? The past – that obscure and sinister period before 1999 – has become a steaming heap of sports trivia. In pubs around Britain punters reflect on the Cuban Missile Crisis, those breathless hours when it seemed that Wolverhampton Wanderers were going to pay the $500 transfer fee of nippy midfielder Miguel 'Mojo' Morales of the Havana Hurricanes, only to back out at the last minute ...

Yes, it's surprisingly unsatisfying being a revisionist historian in a society that thinks the Renaissance is a French station wagon and the Enlightenment is a weight-loss pill. The Englishman is happy to live in the moment, to treasure Jonny

Wilkinson, misspelt name and all, and to dream of taking the Ashes from Australia (a country strangely populated by white English-speaking people who play cricket – doesn't evolution do the darndest things?).

Naturally India's heroics in Sydney this week will cause an eruption of frantic nationalism and patriotism in India, a country that needs nationalism and patriotism the way napalm needs a Zippo. Had India won the Test series, Pakistan could have expected an immediate nuclear strike. By the weekend Indian troops would have crossed into China, and Bangladesh, that lovely brown lake, would have been unwilling host to India's navy, all three rubber-duckies in full battle readiness with twin-mounted flintlock muskets primed and ready.

Mercifully Steve Waugh preserved global stability by batting out a draw, but nevertheless one should expect a series of revelations by New Delhi over the next few weeks: an unpublished concerto found in a Mumbai brothel proving conclusively that the alleged Austrian was in fact called Venkat Amadeus Mozart, a cobbler's son who wrote both *The Magic Hookah* and *The Arranged Marriage of Figaro* when he was fourteen, at least a year younger than any Pakistani prodigy; the Indian Space Agency showing photographs taken by its Habeldas Telescope of what it claims is the goddess Kali, currently dealing death in the X-26B galaxy, 152 light years away.

The past just isn't what it used to be.

Dakar dispatches

Ce n'est pas une pipe, c'est un fag.

January 5, somewhere in southern Mauritania. Michelle, ma petite baguette, I write this by the guttering light of a burning Mitsubishi. The driver will soon be extinguished, and so I must be brief.

The weeping has become incessant. At first it was just the Italian bikers, sobbing into their malfunctioning carburettors (I had not the courage to tell them that mucus and sand form a cement-like compound – the dawn will bring fresh heart-break). But now the night rings with the wailing of Swedes and Australians alike, people unaccustomed to sustained tear-fulness and thus horribly gauche in their efforts. We French cry beautifully, as you know, with a delicate flaring of the nos-tril and a fetching crumpling of the chin: so must Jeanne d'Arc and Robespierre have wept as they faced their doom. But this is getting quite out of hand. If I see one more lachrymose racer I will slap him with my buckskin motoring gloves.

January 6. Am beginning to doubt the wisdom of embark-ing on this rally in a Smart Car. It is très très chic, undoubt-edly, but this afternoon, while rolling end over end down a shallow incline, it occurred to me that I might have to reassess my target of finishing in the top three. Later drove at speed into a camel dropping and had to be towed out by a passing trucker.

January 8. Do not be alarmed, ma petite aubergine, but disaster has overtaken me. Somewhere along the road today, while doing a routine roll, my last carton of Gauloise was flung out into the Sahara. When I regained consciousness I retraced my tracks, following the trail of engine parts I have been shedding all week, but of my cigarettes there was no sign. I could not go far into the desert: there have been rumours of roving bands of Tuareg nomads, armed and irritable and dying for a fag. Apparently local warlords have signed a treaty limiting their cadres to three nicotine patches a day, but no man can live like this. Pray for me.

January 9. *Bonne chance! Formidable!* Found an American driver, won his trust with stirring anecdotes about the American War of Independence and the historical bond between our two proud nations. Told him I had seen a Pizza Hut behind the dunes to our west. He instantly became distastefully homesick and stumbled away into the night, leaving his three cartons of Camels unguarded. Yankee fool! Hid in a small cave until he had gone, then ate twelve of the cigarettes. Will smoke the rest at my leisure.

January 10. Two hundred kilometres east of Wadi Al Qaq came across a South African family in a Combi. Mr Wessels said they were trying to get home to Cape Town after a quick holiday but they'd got lost. Diagnosed his problem at once: he had bought the Paris–Dakar map, rather than the Parys–De Aar version. Later, while sharing the last of my sun-dried gecko with them, I cornered Mrs Wessels and offered her sex for cigarettes. She seemed interested until I clarified that I was the one after cigarettes. Mon petit escargot, do not be angry. I know you would have done the same. *C'est la vie.*

January 13, late. Still no Gauloises. Beginning to see mirages: cigarette-vending machines laughing at me from the shade of date palms. Will conserve strength, travel by night and smoke only six Camel Lights in the late afternoon.

January 16. Forgive messy handwriting, mon petit cul-de-sac, am writing with a spark plug dipped in engine grease. Am terribly cold. Drank last of antifreeze last night. Have had to smoke my gloves and socks. Not bad taste, good draw. My love, remember the good times …

January 19, Bastille Noire, in bed. Mon petit coup d'état, salvation! This morning all seemed lost, with terrible hallucinations: Sophie Marceau and Juliette Binoche were in front of me, naked, with a wheelbarrow full of Lucky Strikes. Yes, my love, in my delirium I would have considered lighting up one of those infernal tubes of filth.

But then the gentle strains of an accordion were heard, and the aroma of garlic singed my nostrils: a patrol of the French Foreign Legion! I have been smoking almost incessantly since this morning. My throat is gloriously raw, my eyes are a lovely shade of red, the corners of my mouth are reassuringly sticky and yellowish, and I have no appetite whatsoever. I have never felt better. Vive la France! Vive le Paris–Dakar!

Simpler, dumber, faster

The author wishes to make it clear that the views expressed in this piece merely reflect his antipathy towards corporate communication, and are in no way a criticism of a financial institution that currently looks after his life savings and administers the bond on his flat. In fact some of his best friends work for Standard Bank, and he thinks their logo is the loveliest shade of blue, and the free pen they gave him, although devoid of ink and somewhat prone to leaving plastic splinters in his hand, has given him hours of pleasure.

The manner in which this newspaper wrote the news before it happened last week ('The Day Rape Was Raped' or, as it turned out, 'The Day After Rape Might Have Been Seduced') had nothing on the frenzy of pre-emptive journalism in the press box at Newlands on Sunday night.

Of course it was fairly safe, with the West Indies on 48 for 8, to suggest in one's lead that the tourists had narrowly lost, but all the same the box was suffused with a bouquet of desperation and horrible cologne.

And so it went almost entirely unnoticed when a stuffed suit delivered an envelope from Standard Bank to every soothsaying scribe, each containing a letter perpetrated by somebody called Victor Nosi.

'The excitement that we hope to bring with the ODI sponsored by Standard Bank, is something that is very important to us,' read the first paragraph, and I realised I was being addressed by someone with the cavalier wit and esprit of a Soviet battery-chicken farmer.

Having thus elegantly set up his argument and numbed his reader's senses with a sharp blow to their intellect, he surged onward. 'We need to put a lot of energy in making sure that the public get a bang for their buck.' Just one bang? Surely a megacorporation like Standard Bank, trampling unchecked across the green pasture that is the South African consumers' inability to complain, can afford to cough up for more than a solitary bang?

But even banks have budgets, so one was all we were going to get. Unashamed at this percussive tightfistedness, Victor continued.

'It is in this spirit that the UCBSA and ourselves are looking at ways of rekindling this part of the game.' Victor's devil-may-care attitude to grammar and sentence construction was starting to take its toll: which spirit, exactly, was he talking about? The spirit of the energy-sapping quest for the singular bang? And which part of the game was firecracker Vic intending to ignite?

Then, apropos of nothing, with haiku-like asceticism, three bullet points appeared. Bullet points have long been the crutch of illiterate executives who never quite got the hang of full stops, but Victor's pithy zingers hung tremulously on the frontier between prose and esoteric performance art.

'That cricket should be fun for families', read the first line, and for a heady moment it seemed possible that I was reading a terribly bad poem penned by Victor in the bath, something like 'That cricket should be fun for families/Is a truth most fertile for homilies.'

'That ODIs are punchy, memorable and', read the second.

Most would suggest that the hanging 'and' was signifying the imminent arrival of a third bullet point, but I propose that this was Victor's realisation of the ultimate failure of language: this prophet of marketing had communed with the god of platitudes, and had been shown The Great Catchphrase. Through tears of joy he had fought to write down what he had seen, unable to express the orgy of greed that had flashed before his eyes. In the end the hanging 'and' was his monument, a testament to his failure to reach his mountaintop, his Volvo convertible.

But he did leave us with an intriguing philosophical problem. Past generations have pondered over how many angels could dance on the point of a needle; but, thanks to Victor, we have this one to mull over: can an event that lasts seven hours, and is usually entirely predictable for the last of those seven hours, be punchy?

'We have committed ourselves that these forthcoming ODIs will be memorable,' wrote Victor. If only he had committed himself earlier. Or been committed. With a final flourish of his quill he bade us 'Keep up the good word' and signed off, leaving one to ponder over which word he meant. 'Pus' is a marvellous word, as are 'lugubrious' and 'moribund', but it seemed unlikely that he wanted these slung around the press box. Perhaps, one wondered, he was hoping for a word that signified good, like 'God' or 'kittens' or 'Isobel Jones'. We'll never know.

But what we do know (because he wrote it under his name) is that Victor Nosi, a man with a tangential relationship with words in general and undoubtedly estranged from syntax, is the Group Communication Director for Standard Bank.

Incidentally, if KPMG needs a new chief accountant, please look me up: I got 47 per cent for Standard Grade maths.

Setting hearts aglow

In early 2004 Greenpeace activists breached the perimeter of South Africa's nuclear power station to make a point about security. No doubt Eskom has since tightened access control by putting a new 'Lumka inja' sign on the farm gate and covering the holes in the chicken wire with good strong lengths of string.

National reconciliation is so much easier when one doesn't have the capacity to vaporise one's former oppressor at the touch of a button. Maybe this was why the previous government cut the wicks off our alleged nuclear arsenal: black majority rule could be envisaged, but not if a luminous mushroom cloud lit up the night over PW Botha's log cabin in the Wilderness.

In non-proliferated hindsight, no nukes has been good news for our little country. Which is why I was perturbed to receive a letter from a major insurance company informing me of a change in the terms of their policies.

Henceforth, I read, I would not be covered for any loss contributed to or arising from (and I quote) ionising, radiations or contamination by radioactivity from any nuclear fuel or from any nuclear waste; nuclear fission or fusion; nuclear explosives or any nuclear weapon; and finally, just in case I didn't have the picture, nuclear waste in any form.

To clarify, the helpful company finished by telling me that I should regard 'combustion' to mean any self-sustaining process of nuclear fission. Thus forewarned against starting my car or lighting a candle lest I obliterate the neighbour-hood, I had to time to peruse the papers. Something about a Koeberg employee whose cancer was hushed up; a snippet about the FBI looking for nuke peddlers in South Africa.

It cast a whole new light, a softly pulsating green one, on the future of the Cape Town nuclear family. Here comes dad, wrapped up snug against the nuclear winter, home from a hard day at the McDonald's Meat Substitute ash heaps where he herds and wrangles cockroaches. Tiddles the golden retriever meets him at the gate. Ah Tiddles, says dad, poor dear Tiddles. Wag your tail while you can because tomorrow you're going into the prototype McMutt burger. Just as well, thinks dad, the poor old pooch was getting a touch of arthritis in her seventh and eighth hips.

Mom is waiting for him in bed, the way she has every day since she got cancer. Luckily she has little Joey to keep an eye on the congenitally joined triplets: Joey might only have one eye, but it's a good one.

Of course this won't happen in Cape Town. Koeberg is safe, because its safety officer said it was, while Greenpeace activists played badminton on its dome. Airport security is likewise impenetrable. If the obese army officer chatting to his girl-friend doesn't get you, and if you somehow slip past the unmanned malfunctioning X-ray machine, and if you go unnoticed by the bipolar customs gang cavity-searching a pensioner who dared to bring golf clubs into the country, then you are bound to be run over in the parking lot.

But let us, in a moment of berserk schadenfreude, think the unthinkable and imagine that South African bureaucrats are capable of error. Does Cape Town have a nuclear contingency plan? And would sport carry on unmolested the morning after, to reassure fidgety citizens across the country? Certainly Cape football teams, slowly disintegrating, would jog out onto a blasted pitch and play to a goalless draw with a deflating ball in a gale saturated with airborne chemicals and poisons, the whole affair smelling like burning rubber. But then, this wouldn't be anything new.

The far more pampered denizens of Newlands might emerge from bunkers built to ward off Perils both Red and Black to see a smouldering ruin surrounded by jagged blocks of concrete, the grass dead and cars shattered for miles around. Ah, they will whisper, Kaizer Chiefs fans have passed this way. Tell me, Nobby old boy, is my vermouth glowing? I can't seem to see, for my monocle has been fused to my eyeball.

Pro surfers, legendarily unflappable, would compare radiation burns as they pushed out into the still-warm swells, contemplatively picking their way through clumps of belly-up fish and the odd smoking shark. Hectic, bru, did you see the flash? It was like, flash! And then it was like, ow! And then I was like, whoa! Totally whack. Dude, are these your toes or are you shedding chipolatas? Nooit. Tastes like chicken.

And of course when the dust settles, sometime around 2050, it will be the sports administrators who are called in as consultants in the most vital part of any nuclear disaster: passing the buck. 'You must understand that redressing the imbalances of the blast is a long process, but we have set up a task team to investigate ...'

Monkey see, monkey do

In February 2004 the Springboks were lured out of their cave by park rangers holding out sugar cubes on the end of long poles, and were taken to meet their new coach ...

New Springbok coach Jake White is a great motivator. He's a student of the game. He's a thinker, a facilitator, a mover, a groover, a philosopher-king. But consider this, in the light of the state of South African rugby: is there anything a modern Springbok coach can do that a trained chimpanzee can't?

Which is not to question Mr White's godlike qualities as expounded by SARFU Director of Rhubarb, Heartthrob Petersen. Indeed, trained chimps can do more than most of us. For instance, they can put whole oranges in their mouths.

They were even trained to pilot space capsules in the Mercury programme. While teaching Percy Montgomery to run in a straight line has its own unique challenges, it can't quite compete with toggling the retrothruster programme sequence during manual oblique re-entry through million-degree plasma.

Frankly, the appointment of White is rampant speciesism, and simian liberation has been dealt a grievous blow. Rugby's administrators will never know the broad sunlit uplands they might have entered had they overcome their outmoded attitudes to the big apes and appointed a 4-year-old chimp called, say, Mr Bojangles.

For one thing, Mr Bojangles would have demanded physical respect from his team. An angry Nick Mallett with brows in full beetle is one thing, but having a coach who can tear one's arm off at the shoulder and who flies into screaming rages every time his favourite beach ball deflates is something else altogether. That's real respect.

Mr Bojangles would work for bananas and sleep in a nest of straw in the SARFU broom-cupboard, freeing the union to divert the millions they would have paid White to lure back the fans. Paying them to watch the Springboks would be a good start.

Naturally there will be nagging doubts about the technical details of a chimp training a squad of rugby players and the possible discrepancy in their motivation. After all, can one trust someone who is paid in fruit to nurture professional sportsmen who play for the love of money? But the question is academic. In a showdown between the Springboks and four chimps, who would you put money on? The prosecution rests, and has a banana.

Mr Bojangles would have been a public relations coup. Just hours into the job he'd have the press corps literally eating out of his hand as he passed around some squashed naartjies and jellybeans: some slightly funky bean-encrusted naartjie pulp couldn't be more insulting to one's intelligence than the average press release.

The press conference begins with Mr Bojangles colouring in Nconde Balfour's tie with a red crayon before searching Brian van Rooyen's ear for termites. He finds only a fishmoth and is dejected. Pensively he sucks on an e-tv microphone.

What are your plans for the future, coach? Mr Bojangles picks his nose and proffers his findings to the SABC camera-man. Fortunately he has been taught some rudimentary sign-language, and quickly settles into his inaugural policy speech, Van Rooyen at his side translating.

'Mr Bojangles says, "Springbok contingency plan happy happy banana, transformation sticky-tape Pronutro." Next question please.'

'What's he saying now?'

'He's signing, "England backline stinky poo rubbish cupcake."'

'Cupcake?'

'All right, gents, that's all for now, the coach needs his nappy changed. Silas, please fetch another cupcake for Mr Bojangles.'

'But he's still signing! What's he saying?'

'"Tri-Nations kitty doll beach-ball cupcake cupcake cupcake." Mr Bojangles, get down from there! I promise your cupcake is on its way. Security, please fetch Mr Bojangles' little sleepy-sleepy darts and the g-u-n. Thank you, gents, that will be all.'

At least the sport's power-brokers in business and government and away from all accountability would finally have a coach that looked the part. After all, they think the players and the public are monkeys, so why not give them one of their own?

Send us your poor,
your crocked, your crooked

In which South Africa's foreign policy seems to be a victim of Aristide development.

Since it became illegal in most European countries to imply that black people or Middle Eastern immigrants are capable of anything other than vibrancy, euphemism has become integral to law-enforcement in the West.

In briefings around Britain, bobbies are handed curiously grey identikits, bearing in tiny print at the bottom the legend, 'Any similarity between persons of any identifiable race group, living or dead, is strictly coincidental. All racial profiling resulting from this picture is purely a result of the racism inherent in all whites.'

Indeed, Islamist suicide bombers present the greatest threat to European spokesmen unable to call a spade anything but a cuddly friend who loves digging. 'Islamist' might tick off new German voters, 'suicide' has so much negative baggage, and 'bombers' invariably reminds one of the vicious unprovoked attacks on Dresden and Hiroshima by British and American imperialism in the 1940s. No, in the future it seems possible that we will start hearing about civilians on buses falling victim to 'Persian pyrotechnics'.

Already England's top police brass refer unflinchingly to 'Caribbean gun crime', transforming London's slummier neighbourhoods into a perennial fiesta of sun, sand, reggae and tracer bullets.

Caribbean gun crime is reportedly one of Jamaica's busiest exports. The island is lousy with weapons, and it even had a few before South Africa's shipment of arms arrived this week. One only needs to look over modern reworkings of calypso classics to see how times have changed. For instance there's the evergreen 'Tally Me Bazooka' ('Ammo! Aaaaammo! Daylight come and me gotta reload/Six and seven and eight and whump!/Daylight come and me gotta reload') and the old favourite 'Jamaica Farewell' ('Down the way where the nights are gay/and the sun shines daily off me 9-mil Glock').

Those weapons were of course headed for Haiti after our government decided that what the island needed was more guns. Alas, the hardware was waylaid by the tallymen of Jamaica, and President Jean-Bertrand Aristide grabbed his toothbrush and put the Atlantic, Guinea and Gabon between himself and his revolting populace.

Aristide's plaintive and brief scratching at Pretoria's door last week made one reflect on those unfortunate souls who are forced to set sail for our shores, and whether it would be cheaper to torpedo them in open water or just to lay mines on the high-water mark. But it should also have alerted shrewd sports administrators to the lucrative possibilities of harbouring asylum-seekers. After all, our sport is symbolised by a quick buck, albeit a horned one.

It's not as if we don't already host disgraceful sportsmen. Just look at the Cats. Losing Premier Division managers could easily be lured into hiding somewhere adequate like Clifton if we played our cards right. Last week a report was published in this newspaper about managers receiving death threats, having half-bricks lobbed through their windows, and being beaten into comas. But not all football fans are as restrained in expressing their devotion to their club, and if managers remain aloof (nothing infuriates a Scouser like trying to belittle someone in a coma) the terraces can turn nasty. You'll never walk alone, sing Liverpool's faithful to manager Gerard Houllier, but one can't help wondering if there are lines to read between: walk alone, to the corner café for example, and you'll never walk again.

Of course the richest pickings for our team of sports amnesty scouts would be North American. Canadian sprinter Ben Johnson's biceps used to be the size of his head. Then he started taking steroids, making one wonder how a human brain could fit inside that streamlined tennis ball of a cranium. But then he did think that nobody would be suspicious if his body inflated like a parade float just before the Seoul Olympics, so perhaps the tennis-ball brain question answers itself.

Having settled Ben in a cosy Fancourt crib they could approach Cincinnati Reds slugger Pete Rose, excommunicated for gambling on baseball games, or perhaps that lead-pipe-wielding sugarplum fairy from hell, ice-skater Tonya Harding, who had rival Nancy Kerrigan's kneecap tenderised in the name of fair play.

But it takes shame to make people run, so don't expect any immediate arrivals. Without the slightest trace of irony, Rose is launching his umpteenth bid to get into baseball's Hall of Fame, while Harding has decided to follow her heart and is making a name for herself as a prize-fighter.

Well, we'll always have the Cats.

The cycle of violence is
over for another year

*A woman needs a man like a fish needs a bicycle. And a man needs
a bicycle like a woman needs a fish.*

In 2002 a study by the CIA revealed that the most dangerous
roads in the world belong to Iran. The announcement dealt a
severe blow to the Iranian tourism board, then just launching
its 'Hey, at least we're not Afghanistan' campaign, and for the
following eighteen months the annual influx of international
visitors to Tehran halved to five.

Imagine the jubilation, then, when a few dozen tourists
arrived in Tehran this year. The fact that they came with
Geiger counters, fallout suits and awkward questions did little
to dampen the jollification; and besides, nervous officials
might have argued, if things got messy they could always be
sent on a little sightseeing drive down Route 1 (turn left out
of Tehran, keep on until you hit the fourteenth century). Bad
roads aren't all bad.

It goes a long way towards explaining why Iranians kept
hijacking airliners in the 1980s. There comes a point in every
man's life, usually when he is nursing a Peugeot 404 with no
brakes along a precipice in Asia Minor, chickens rioting in the
glove compartment and a lugubrious goat duct-taped to the
hood, that he wonders if there's an easier way to travel. Like in
the cockpit of a British Airways jumbo, say.

It is possible that the report is now outdated, that fresh hells await motorists in different parts of the world. For instance, Iran would surely struggle to compete with the unique challenges of driving an open-topped Humvee up the Saddam the Magnificent Interstate Superhighway near Tikrit singing 'This Land Is My Land'.

But as Ted Kennedy said en route to Chappaquiddick, bad roads do not a bad driver make. It takes more than a rutted Iranian riverbed-cum-highway or an Iraqi shooting gallery to push motorists to the limits of endurance. For that, you need to be in Cape Town on the weekend of the Argus Cycle Tour.

JM Coetzee once suggested that the bicycle is the only non-harmful machine devised by the West. As opposed to vicious machines like, say, alarm clocks. But it's true: bicycles are non-harmful. Left alone in their natural habitat they struggle to reproduce, tending instead to fall over and rust. But man must meddle. We found atoms, we split them, and the result was nuclear bombs. We found bicycles, we sat on them, and the result was cyclists. And until the world unites to sign a Velocipede Non-Proliferation Treaty, we are doomed to the kind of mania the Argus race provokes.

The race itself is rarely an inconvenience. Capetonians pass the day in their basements, absentmindedly playing backgammon by lamplight, reassuring tearful children, slipping away unobtrusively to re-check the deadbolts on the door. At noon a caged budgie is pushed out of a ventilation shaft on the end of a long stick, and if it comes back without a spoke through its eye or Spandex burns, the day can resume.

But it is the days leading up to the event that lead to the trauma, when that particular mindset of the training cyclist – a disgruntled and stubborn self-righteousness, like a cow grazing halfway up Runway 1 at Heathrow – is given free rein. The Argus of Greek myth was a hundred-eyed giant, mercilessly teased at school (a brief stint with bifocals earned him the nickname 'Two-hundred-eyes') but unparalleled as a watchman. And one might enjoy the irony inherent in naming an orgy of tunnel vision after an omniscient being if one weren't so busy dodging oblivious cyclists.

Up every available incline, round every blind corner, these self-propelled blind-spots wobble and veer. Their rumps, a year out of the saddle and grown mutinous through flirtations with chocolate éclairs, shimmer over the tarmac, zeppelins playing tag in a Spandex sky. Try to pass them, and they heave towards starboard brandishing their water bottles; creep behind them, and they gesture furiously for you to pass, their agitation sending them careening across the lane towards an onrushing petrol tanker.

But perhaps all of this is motorists' sour grapes. Perhaps the white knuckles on the steering wheel and feverish fancies about the physics of winding a bicycle chain around a human neck are simple jealousy.

After all, the cyclist can demand the full protection of the rules of the road without obeying a single one of them. So when push comes to shove, halfway up Suikerbossie, he's had his chocolate éclair and eaten it.

Ah, look at all the lonely people

Nobody got this one, and in the end it proved to be the Eleanor Rigby of the collection. Frankly it's only in here as an excuse to hammer the Swiss again.

Here's what we know about Eleanor Rigby. We know that at some stage, probably on a Saturday afternoon, she picked up the rice in a church where a wedding had been. Apparently she lived in a dream. We know that she waited at the window, and that she had a jar by the door, since this is where she kept her face. We still don't know whom it was for.

We also know that she died in the church and was buried along with her name, and that nobody came. The grave-digging duties were carried out by a Father McKenzie.

But what did Ms Rigby usually do between putting on her face and getting stuck into the rice? What about the other six or seven hours in her waking day? Certainly, there was a fair amount of waiting by the window, but if she had the motivation to open the jar, apply her face, select a rice receptacle, go to the church and get down on all fours, she was far from catatonic. Miserable, yes, but mobile.

It is here that Ms Rigby's prospective biographer must pause and ask: what do depressed, lonely, abandoned, socially inadequate people do?

Obviously most go and live in Switzerland, where they congregate on the shores of Lake Geneva on chilly autumn evenings to skip gold coins out into the dusk, recognising in the slowly diminishing ripples the onrushing reality of their deaths. Then they turn for home to dine alone on swan, mink stew and grief.

But not all losers are resigned. Some can simulate enthusiasm, cutting out and cataloguing John Pilger columns into folders labelled 'Somebody should do something', 'Too right' and 'Bloody Jews'. Sometimes, if the light is dim enough for them to go outside, they even dabble in sports. And on very rare occasions, emboldened to reckless exhibitionism by a satisfying heart-to-heart with the talking clock, they invent new ones.

Take pickleball. Take it and put it in a bag and hit for an hour with pipes. This sport is tennis played on a tiny court with a perforated ball. According to the US Pickleball Association, the game 'builds self-esteem in youngsters' and 'provides competitive competition for active athletes'.

Clearly American youngsters need all the help they can get, in this case a ball that moves slowly enough for obese preteens to get their flab rolling in formation before the drifting orb has bounced twice. The sport's degrees of competition must also be terribly reassuring to children oozing mayonnaise from every pore: if competitive competition is too strenuous, you can always opt for something like shooting fish in a barrel with an assault rifle.

But not surprisingly it is the Swiss who have shown the greatest inability to grasp the point of sport by inventing the awful pantomime known as tchoukball. Not to be confused with the Australian sport of chookball in which chickens are randomly kicked over fences, tchoukball was invented by a Dr Hermann Brandt in the 1960s as a result 'of a critical scientific study of the most popular team sports'.

According to Geneva's leading tchoukball club, the impossibly dull doctor noticed that most sports injuries 'resulted from performing movements inadequate with the individual's physiology, as well as from the many forms of aggression present in some sports'.

Clearly appalled at the elitist and murderous cult of sport in general, firecracker Brandt set about levelling the playing field to prevent asthmatic cheese-tasters from Basel from tripping over their shoelaces. His first drafts never saw the light of day: walking rugby with a beach ball, played on a shag-pile carpet; high jump over an earbud held aloft by two marshmallows; bathtub waterpolo with a balloon for a ball and soapsuds as opposition.

But in the end his brainchild was born, a runt bastard of volleyball and pelota, and he rejoiced that it was 'characterised by the suppression of any form of corporal aggression between the opponents'.

Next to Herr Dokter Brandt, Eleanor Rigby was a biker slut on crack, but perhaps she too indulged in sport. Maybe even tchoukball. And if this was the case, it's not impossible that she met Hermann, perhaps even invited him to church on a date.

And so the questions remain. Did Eleanor Rigby die from complications after slipping on rice, or was she bored to death one cold evening by a Swiss blancmange?

All the lonely people, where do they all come from? And how many of them play pickleball?

Ill met by Moonlight

This was triggered by a rumour that a considerable number of the great-grandchildren of the Nazi High Command are now living the good life in Cape Town. I am consoled by the thought of the master race stepping in Tamboerskloof poodle turds and having its flaxen coif annihilated by the south-easter. Today zer Bo-Kaap, tomorrow zer liposuction clinic.

It was all unspeakably divine for Greta von Ribbentrop, formerly of Buenos Aires and Lüderitz, and now of Oranjezicht. She had found that in Africa people did not ask nasty pointed questions about the granddaughters of high-ranking Nazis, and she was free to enjoy her extensive collection of French and Russian art, in the family since 1943, in peace.

It was her first Met, and as the days drew nearer she could no longer contain her excitement and began to belabour her chauffeur around the head with an ornamental riding crop given her as a christening present. Suddenly she gave a shrill cry, her nose pressed to the glass.

'Gustav! Look! Blacks! Stealing horses!'

'Those are their owners, ma'am,' said Gustav. 'Observe, if you will, their tuxedos.'

'I'm sure I've seen that one on *Crimestop*. He looks so familiar!'

'He's the Deputy President, ma'am.'

'It's still so confusing,' sighed Greta as they swung through the gates of Kenilworth Racecourse. A fresh breeze was ripping in off the South Atlantic, and someone's hat – a crimson replica of Westminster Abbey – went rolling away through the gathering crowd, breaking legs and hips before it smashed through a brick wall and was gone.

Her own hat, a scale model of Cologne Cathedral, had deflated somewhat during the ride and needed some attention with a bottle of compressed air. While Gustav reinforced two of its flying buttresses with duct tape and hairspray, Greta took in the scene around her.

'What I need is an Irishman or a Jew to tell me which horses to bet on,' she mused. 'They know about that sort of thing.' Just then somebody walked past who looked ideal. She clutched his sleeve. 'I say, you look just like Shylock. Are you a Jew?'

Gustav hastily disentangled himself from the hat and bowed. 'Miss Greta von Ribbentrop, may I introduce you to Mr Trevor Manuel, the Minister of Finance?'

'Finance, eh? So you *are* a Jew!' she exclaimed, clapping her hands together with joy. The man excused himself graciously and sprinted for the cover of some distant parasols.

There was still no sign of her girlfriends, and so she took a tour of the grounds while she waited. It was terribly exotic. There were students from the university all wearing hired suits, vomiting spectacularly behind the beer tent, and their dates, a miserable gaggle of blonde 15-year-olds who had stolen their mothers' makeup in an effort to look 18. However, a fine layer of red dust and an hour's worth of sweat had conspired to leave them looking like 62-year-old Neapolitan prostitutes.

Suddenly there was a thundering sound, and some people began to cheer. A student cheered and then vomited, and then cheered some more. The public address bellowed.

'And they're off,' it said, 'and it's Flaming Goitre leading Armadillo Lust by a length, and it's Glue On Legs closing fast on the outside but it's Moonlight Apocalypse making his move on Armadillo Lust and Manchurian Chastity is fading fast, it's Moonlight Apocalypse and Flaming Goitre, it's, it's —' There was a gasp and a thud. 'And Moonlight Apocalypse is down! He's fallen and it's Glue On Legs by a nose!'

Greta's phone rang. It was Adelheid Himmler and Heike Goering, just pulling in. Adelheid was hysterical. 'The blacks are stealing horses in the parking lot!' she yelled. 'And Heike's not getting out of the car because she says there's real poop lying around that might get on her Manolo Blahniks.'

'Come and find me,' said Greta, spying a sign that read 'Retired horses this way'. 'I'm at the retirement paddock. It's sponsored by a dog-food company, you can't miss the sign. Moonlight Apocalypse has just arrived. They're measuring his haunches and there's a sort of mincing machine standing in the corner.'

'I can't see you,' said Adelheid. 'Is that you? Oh, no, that's a hat-stand. Oh god, Heike's fur sombrero just blew off.' Greta craned to see what looked like a small grizzly bear flying north over some pine trees. 'Is that you kissing a boy behind the beer tent? Oh, that's Heike. Stop it! Come here!'

Gustav suddenly appeared at her side. 'Your hat, ma'am. I'm afraid there is a beetle in the nave and the south bell-tower has been punctured by a bee, but the rest is splendid.'

'Oh Gustav!' she cried. 'Thank God you're here. I'm so tired. I've seen so many things. Take me home.'

The rain in Bahrain goes mainly down the drain

Whoever said you can't buy class clearly doesn't follow Formula One. Once upon a time a chap required a stately home in Kent, a piece of German anti-aircraft artillery lodged in his hip, and a weakness for Brazilian strippers just to get a glimpse of a pit-lane. Today all it takes is a chequebook and a dodgy human rights record.

Negotiations over the granting of a Grand Prix to Bahrain were apparently as tough as a Saudi prince's hands. The Minister for State-Sponsored Decadence, reclining on a migrant labourer, gave Bernie Ecclestone his final offer. 'Bernie, light of my eye and song of my heart, can I peel you another grape?'

In the past I have slandered the unbearable soul-destroying misery that is Port Elizabeth; but after the last weekend the residents of that blighted hovel by the scum-flecked sea can lift their heads and say that they no longer inhabit the world's ugliest place. That honour is now reserved for the citizens of Bahrain.

Watching the Formula One circus whiz round a giant box of kitty litter with some tar smeared across it, one had to wonder where the £100 million spent on the track's construction had gone. Palm trees cost about ten bucks a go, so there's fifty spent. And the glue needed to keep it all from lifting off and blowing into the Red Sea probably cost about a thousand. I smell books cooking.

The French attempt to ban the wearing of religious apparel by Muslim immigrants has predictably set the chattering classes chattering, but somehow nobody chatters much about Western women in the Middle East being expected to shroud themselves like the ghouls they're considered. In this climate of one-eyed sartorial fanaticism it was always going to be tricky for Bernie to line pits with the usual half-naked nymphs, collagen and silicone straining at the seams.

Perhaps it is time the West followed the example of Brazil and declared the bikini an item of holy significance. However, in a magnanimous gesture of international camaraderie, the state allowed women team-members to wear overalls and to make eye contact with their colleagues who weren't their brother/father/uncle. But multicultural tolerance only goes so far, leaving the mystery of what exactly it was that was spraying out of the champagne bottles on the podium.

Sparkling grape juice is one possibility, but there's always the danger of leaving a magnum of the stuff standing in 40-degree heat and its fermenting into something satanic. Sparkling water is out of the question, since all the water in the Emirates is carefully rationed between the irrigation of golf courses and ornamental fountains depicting Saddam Hussein pissing on the White House. No, it must have been the only liquid they can spare in Bahrain: petrol. Good thing no one lit a celebratory cigar.

The addition of this race to the Grand Prix calendar will reportedly go some way towards patching up relations between the region and the West, implying that if everyone is rich and fat, nobody feels like blowing up anyone else. And while on the topic of repressive regimes being bribed with lucrative sporting events, China now also has its own Grand Prix.

Naturally the concept of competition will have to be explained to the Beijing politburo as they shuffle into the hospitality suite, but they should catch on fairly quickly if analogies are drawn between Ferrari and China on the one hand, and McLaren and Taiwan on the other.

Given the Chinese penchant for over-enthusiastic emulation, known in the West as piracy, motoring enthusiasts will be awaiting the launch of surprisingly affordable Chinese-produced Ferraris at the end of the year, 50 cc engines mounted in plastic chassis screaming up the byways of the Orient. Fans can also look forward to owning their own genuine original entirely real racing helmet signed by Mikel Shoomucha himself, made in the factory at Modena, Hong Kong.

Bernie has paid someone to make his bed, and now he must sleep in it. The sport of motor racing has turned the corner into a world of political expediency and global demand, and in a decade Bahrain will seem as tame as Belgium. What thrills await the faithful: dodging Datsuns mounted with machine guns on the home straight of the Democratic Congolese Grand Prix; drivers fuming in the pits in Nicaragua, waiting for their crews to be ransomed by religious crack dealers; the late-night two-hour 800-kilometre sprint in a straight line through Chechnya, illuminated by mortar bursts.

Will they last? Will the Libyan Grand Prix be a success or will Muammar Gaddafi be visited by an angel in a dream who will tell him to hold all the drivers hostage until he is granted the Soccer World Cup?

It's go, go, go indeed.

Hot Goss as Posh in Slag Totty Bonk Row with Love-Rat Becks

This got me my one and only lamppost placard, which makes me think I'd be far more famous by now if I'd gone into tabloid journalism. Unfortunately I'm overqualified for our local rags because I can chew with my mouth closed.

Posh Spice was gutted when she discovered that Becks had snogged a slag. She suddenly wanted to vomit. If only she hadn't renounced all that at Anorexics Anonymous. She counted to ten and ate a celery stick. The news had been read to her, since those tabloid editorials can be so text-heavy. And because her eyes were sealed shut when tears mixed her mascara into a cement-like compound. Her ordeal had only just begun.

For those whose subscriptions to *The Sun* have, like mine, lapsed, the hot goss is as follows. Becks snogged a totty, but told Posh it was bosh that he'd shagged the slag. Posh said 'Gosh!' at a posh thrash where she was splashing dosh about. She copped one at Becks, who sobbed. Posh blubbed too. The dirty love-rat denied hot pash on the physio bench, but then came the Becks sex text tester.

Disappointingly none of the reports billed the SMS conversation as 'Becks' Totty Sham Hots-Purr'. Or 'Man United with Posh's Fist'. They don't write tabloid headlines like they used to.

As for the text messages themselves, their content seemed to crouch somewhere between 'Soft, what burglar through yonder window breaks?' and 'Wanna breed?' Two people who have dedicated their waking hours to kicking balls and rubbing hamstrings respectively were always going to struggle with the rhyming couplets at the end of their sonnets.

The Beckhams, being middle-class people treading water in a giant aquarium full of money, will probably stay together for the sake of their children. Of course if they'd really had their children's best interests at heart, they would never have conceived them to start with, but that's another story.

So now Mrs Beckham has joined the vast, politely smiling army of women married to men regarded as role models presumably because of their skill at rolling about with models in hotel rooms.

Let's play a game. Name your favourite living sportsman between the age of 20 and 30. Now pick a number between four and ten. Subtract one from that number if he has a girlfriend, and halve it if he's married. Multiply it by five if he's an Australian Rules player, and by ten if he's American. That's how many groupies he beds on an average tour.

Of course he has a trophy wife, but trophy wives are for producing babies and taking to award dinners. He wouldn't dream of using her for unmentionables. After all, as Tony Soprano explained, she kisses his children goodnight with that mouth. No, there comes a time in every top athlete's life as he begins to mature as a person when he realises that he is demonstrating his love and respect for his wife by indulging in all-night e-fuelled vodka-soaked romps with 19-year-old twins. He's doing it for her.

Shaun Pollock seems something of a comedown after all

that, and certainly he is one of that breed of Natalians that think 'e' is a sound you put before all words when you want blacks to understand you: please remember to pack away e-hose when you're done watering e-lawn. But there was something downright sinister about a recent *You* magazine feature on the Pollocks and their new baby daughter.

Shaun looked jolly proud of his little girl, and Mrs Shaun looked jolly proud of Shaun and the porcelain ducks he has provided her for her old age. But if one tallied up the facts provided about the couple, one found the following: Shaun is happy, Mrs Shaun is happy that Shaun is happy. Shaun is looking forward to spending time with his daughter, Mrs Shaun is happy about that too. Shaun looks like Archie and plays cricket. Mrs Shaun is pretty and has babies. Baby Shaun is a girl, so probably won't be a fast bowler. But maybe Mrs Shaun can crank out a boy to set the world to rights.

A happy family scene, no doubt, with normal conversations and the odd fight. But to *You* and its readers – and who amongst us can honestly claim that they have never sat on the loo and started with the celeb goss at the back first? – the piece was about a sportsman, his leggy greenhouse, and a cute disappointment.

Lock up your daughter, dye her blonde tresses brown, and pray for the day that Prince Valium the accountant pulls up in his slightly dinged Camry to woo her. It's her only hope.

Brushing up their short game

I'd been to the fillems on the evening of my deadline, and somehow nothing quite seemed to matter in the world beyond Scarlett Johansson's prehensile lips.

'There's action, and then some. But when it's drizzly spring-time in Delft, with that familiar aroma of cheese, mildewed sheets and raw sewage festering under a leaden sky, you know it's time for world-class golfing action. Yes folks, welcome to the 400th Dutch Masters, live from crappy Holland! And a warm welcome to my co-anchor, Bob Weinberger.'

'Thanks, Chuck, great to be back. Boy, there's nothing like it, is there? The polders, the cows, the clogs. Just this morning I was cutting the complimentary cheese in my hotel bathroom, and thinking how much we love this tournament.'

'We sure do, Bob. Of course this year's Dutch Masters is, as always, brought to you by Peter Stuyvesant: just one draw and you're hooked. I sure do like them golf puns. So, take us through the line-up.'

'Well, this year we've got a couple of new faces. Gerrit Dou has been making waves on the Leiden tour, and he's shooting up the money list thanks to big wins at the Queen Christina Open in Stockholm and the Medici Classic in Florence. Some controversy about that last win, though, Chuck: it turned out his *Lady at Her Toilet* didn't feature an actual toilet scene.'

'That must have come as quite a disappointment to "Kinky" Cosimo de' Medici, Bob. Well, moving on, we've got young

Anthony van Dyck and veteran Peter Paul Rubens. What's the word on these two?'

'Gee, Chuck, I don't know. I guess they've just never kind of kicked on. Both brilliant golfers, no question, and there was a time they looked set to take the green jacket off Rembrandt, but in recent seasons they've maybe just been a little too focused on their driving and concepts of divinity. Huge shots, often with biblical themes, and I reckon they just forgot about the short game. Rubens especially. He tore up the European tour for years, looked totally unstoppable after *The Apotheosis of Henry IV and the Proclamation of the Regency of Maria de' Medici on May 14, 1610*, but then I guess he kind of got the yips.'

'Sorry to interrupt, Bob, but we've got a disturbance down at the first tee, a huge crowd of kids, maybe fifty or sixty … oh, it's the Vermeer family. And there's Jan himself, stud golfer of Delft and mullet pioneer. Gee, they sure love him here.'

'And he loves them right back, Chuck. Those fifty kids are just the ones we know about. But we were talking about short games, and this guy has the best short game in the world. Sure, he's pedantic and slow, but holy crap, what a winner.'

'Is it true that *Girl with a Pearl Earring* was originally called *Girl with a Perlemoen Nose-Stud?*'

'Sure is, Chuck, and let me tell you it was a mess, that big old green sack of slime hanging off that pretty little face. Luckily he changed caddies, and the rest is history.'

'We've just had a viewer e-mail us a question about the big white ruffs that everyone's wearing today, both the golfers and their models. Is this some sort of seventeenth-century Flemish fashion item, Bob?'

'Great question, but no. Those are just to keep people from licking their stitches.'

'Such vibrant customs and sanitary habits here in the Low Countries. And now to the guy that everyone's been talking about all week. Okay, Bob, tell me this. He's got the longest drive in the game, a putter that's always on fire, unrivalled brush technique, he's won about half of the last 400 Dutch Masters, he's second in the money list behind Pablo Picasso, and yet those who know him say he's a deeply unhappy man. Why is Rembrandt van Rijn looking so glum?'

'Well, Chuck, it's hard to speculate, but I'd say it has something to do with his wife and three of his four kids dying. He's also just declared bankruptcy. And you must remember that life can't be easy for someone whose middle name is Harmenszoon. I mean, think about it. It rhymes with "poon" and "loon".'

'And "spoon", Bob. And "June".'

'Yes, but those aren't really ...'

'And "noon" and "croon".'

'Never mind. The point is, I think his performance at the Masters last year, where he carded a self-portrait and *St Paul at His Writing Desk*, showed someone deeply aware of his own failings, and unflinchingly documenting his misery. He still putted like a son of a bitch, though. Let's join the action on the first tee ...'

Kom, laat ons bid

Insiders said our World Cup Bid was a done deal. Still, it seems we left nothing to chance …

The Egyptian delegation had just left, and the FIFA officials were beside themselves with delight. The complimentary fly-swatters shaped like the Nile Delta had been a resounding success, and the complimentary flies, encrusted around the complimentary date cookies, added an air of glamorous authenticity that everyone agreed really topped off a splendid presentation.

They had just finished marking out a racetrack on the rug and were winding up their new clockwork camels when a head popped around the door.

'About bloody time,' said Sepp Blatter's masseur, Monsieur Defarge, who was also the senior bid adjudicator. 'Three sugars in mine. Leave the donuts on the desk and close the door on the way out.'

'I'm Danny Jordaan,' said the head. 'The South African bid delegation?'

'Go away and come back in ten minutes,' said M Defarge.

Ten minutes later the mood was sombre. Three camels had bogged down in the rug and disintegrated, and the fourth had haemorrhaged a mainspring that had shot it, hump and all, over the bar fridge and out of the window. Some complimentary flies were floating face down in a glass of sherry. Jordaan and his advance team were ushered in.

'What have you got for us?' asked FIFA's Director of Acquisitions, lugubriously thumbing the already-rusting head of his camel.

'Well,' said Jordaan, 'there's a presentation, and then there are a few people …'

'No, I mean, what have you got for us? Ostrich-egg clocks, bushman thumb-pianos, that sort of thing. Pierre here is awfully fond of those Zulu girls, the ones with no clothes on. I don't suppose you brought one of those?'

'I'm sorry, we didn't think …'

'Oh, just get on with it.'

Two pages and six pie-charts into the presentation, things were looking grim. Irvin Khoza kept clutching at his tie-knot and coughing, and M Defarge was playing Snake on his cellphone. It was time for Operation Witblits Koeksister. Jordaan gave the pre-arranged signal – a rapid clicking of his fingers while peering over his shoulder at the door – and Charlize Theron entered.

'Mr Defarge, gentlemen,' she said, her Benonican accent crisp as an East Rand winter morning and twice as smoky. 'This bid means the world to me, because it means the world to my country. Like all my fellow South Africans I love this great sport, this noble game, and if you give your support to South Africa, we have the human spirit, the love, to make this the greatest ice-hockey world championship ever.' A tear gleamed in the corner of her eye and then plopped onto the cookie crumbs at her feet.

'That's what I'm talking about!' cried M Defarge, hammering on the table-top with a shoe. 'Damn good presentation. Especially the dress. Call me.'

Jordaan had been to enough Cosatu meetings to know what Iscor shop stewards always said: strike while the iron is hot. In a flash Charlize was gone and a stately figure appeared at the door.

'Holy crap!' cried the panel. 'It's Morgan Freeman!'

'Actually it's Nelson Mandela,' said Jordaan.

'Who?'

"Do the little dance, Madiba. The little shuffly one."

M Defarge yawned. 'That's a dance? Looks more like the Tin Man from *The Wizard of Oz* before he got oiled.'

'But it's Nelson Mandela!'

Defarge shrugged. 'Look, Danny, he seems like a nice old man, but let's be honest: he's no Justin Timberlake, is he now? I mean I think it's lovely about the Nobel Prize and all that, but there's no X-factor, you know.'

'He's an ex-political prisoner.'

'Don't get cute, son. Not with me. I'll be frank, you should have got Morgan Freeman.'

A large man in dark glasses appeared through a side door and started helping Jordaan pack up his documents.

'I've got FW de Klerk out there!' cried Jordaan as he was lifted to his feet. 'How about Desmond Tutu?'

'Sure, pal, great. An apartheid politician and a stand-up comic in a cassock. Top stuff. Hey, next time bring a crack whore and a monkey with a banjo.'

Outside, the sun was setting. Soon the lepers of Zurich would be starting their nightly hunt for cheese offcuts. With a final effort Jordaan wrenched himself free and flung himself back through the doors.

'Did I mention that we expect visitors to spend around a billion pounds in two months?'

There was a long silence, and then M Defarge offered him a date cookie. 'Let's talk,' he said.

Chorus of dissent

Tautology is invaluable and priceless to affirming yes-men. And they also repeat themselves a lot.

Awkward questions were asked in Pretoria this week over how South Africa won its Football World Cup bid without consulting a single praise-singer.

Disturbing evidence of an entirely spoken bid presentation has come to light, and speculation is rife that the bid team had neither a praise-singing contingency plan nor an emergency backup ceremonial leopard tail.

An unnamed source close to the South African Football Association said this week that he was 'pretty sure' Thabo Mbeki and Nelson Mandela 'could have strung some halalas together if things got tight' but declined to comment on why no qualified praise-singers had been included in the bid team.

It was just the latest twist in the decades-long saga that has gripped filmmakers, novelists, oral historians and other degenerates over the years.

As most people know by now, the praise-singing fraternity was in tatters by the late 1990s. A splinter group, claiming that hip-hop slam oratory was the future of feudal sycophancy, and calling for a blanket ban on all similes involving elephants and thunder, split away to form the Black Liberated Azanian Praise Singers' Interim Executive, or BLAPSIE. Those moderates left behind, who still clung naïvely to iambic pentameter and refused to have their leopard tails fitted with Velcro for easy detachment, named their new association the People's Organisation of Praise Singers, or POOPS.

A strained truce was arranged, and despite sporadic outbreaks of purple prose and one ugly incident involving a hyperbole and a panga, it seemed that the old hostilities were over.

But last year saw a sudden upsurge in verbosity and redundancy as fresh unrest broke out with POOPS demanding that the Scorpions investigate claims that BLAPSIE was lacing POOPS jackal-skin codpieces with Deep Heat.

Days later, BLAPSIE accused POOPS of industrial espionage, producing surveillance footage of POOPS cadres tampering with top-secret calabashes and flywhisks. In a statement that lasted a shade over nine hours, POOPS denied the claims, saying that just as the ant accuses the elephant of causing the thunder to roar, being small of wit, so BLAPSIE sought to hang a false fruit, a rotten fruit (rotten like the fruit that lies upon the ground having rotted and fallen, because it is rotten, the fruit) upon the towering branches of the baobab.

But this week the bickering came to dramatic halt as the newly formed Praise Singers' Youth Council Head Office (PSYCHO) demanded to know why no card-carrying praise-singers had been selected to accompany the World Cup bid team to Switzerland.

Citing its own development programme, where Young Apprentice Praise Singers (YAPS) are moulded for the future, PSYCHO said it was outraged that the bid was awarded to the South African delegation without even a brief performance by a promising Yap.

'Our Grade Three Yaps had been preparing a short presentation for months,' said a PSYCHO spokes-singer. 'Now their little hearts are crying, crying like the rain when it rains.' He said the children would have read from their workbook, *Sipho, Thandi and Spot Go to the Supermarket and Praise the Bag-Packers*.

Meanwhile a veteran praise-singer warned his younger colleagues to pace themselves over the next few weeks. Speaking on condition of anonymity, he revealed that his own career had been ruined by an obsessive admiration for Nelson Mandela, resulting in a medical condition known as Excessive Praise Singing Over Madiba Salivary and Laryngeal Tissue Stress, or EPSOM SALTS.

'Halala Danny Jordaan!' he croaked. 'Halala Madiba and Thabo! Halala everybody, but let us remember that six years is a long time, long like the road that leads from the place you have been to the place you are going to, there and back again, like a road, like a snake, yebo.

'Yes, they conquered the mighty peaks of Switzerland without the crutch of Eurocentric skis, those little planks of globalisation that level the playing fields but leave deep scars behind in the pure snow. Yes, they are bringing a great treasure home, the Oscar of Oscars, the Heinz Winkler of Heinz Winklers.

'But now it is time to build like the termite. With our spit and our red sand we will build. The stadiums will be strong like a hippo, and round like the moon, and have lots of chairs like Yankee Stadium where the Yankee stalks. Nca, it will be glorious!'

Asked what the World Cup meant to him, he said he was hoping to find a job on a construction site somewhere.

But is it art?

In which I am removed from the National Gallery's mailing list, and the sports pages of the 'Mail&Guardian' are turned into a papier-mâché model of a womb, into which a roast chicken filled with nails is inserted as a protest against the hegemony of ingestion. It is a very powerful piece, until it begins to go vrot.

Last week a part of Charles Saatchi's collection of modern art was burnt to cinders. For the second time in a million years, fire has rescued our species.

For two decades the obsolescent mimics of the Young British Artists have delighted in ridiculing the provincialism and crass literalness of middle-class viewers. While picking their noses in public and marvelling at the originality of their snot, they managed to short-circuit common sense, declaring that anyone who suspected them of being charlatans (or, more generously, dullards) was simply justifying their shrill indictment of everything.

The mind that is attracted to games with originality usually hasn't experienced very much more than divorce and boredom, and perhaps theirs had never been introduced to stories about emperors and new clothes.

But what does the middle-class philistine say about this purging fire when his every utterance damns him to further oafishness? Well, for starters: nya nya nya nya nya. Then he might remark on the chiaroscuro effect of the flames on the warehouse walls, the bold new medium of ash on concrete with a hint of fire-retardant foam. Perhaps if he hadn't been patronised for so long he might try to be sympathetic. But probably he just wouldn't care.

Those whose nerve failed them at Sotheby's and who couldn't fork out £40 000 for a tent or a toilet seat or a half-brick on a banana peel might safely bet that amount on the probability that no sporting art returned to ashes and dust last week. More's the pity.

Like the uncle with the gothic appendix scar and the clammy hands, bad artworks featuring sport are grafted on to families and impossible to ditch. There it hangs, acrylic thick as toothpaste starting to flake, fishmoths cavorting in its immense baroque frame: thirty stick-figures on a virulent green rectangle struggling over a disturbingly rhomboid ball, a bloody sun (roughly round, if you ignore the right-angle) sinking towards what might be Table Mountain.

But one mustn't be too harsh. How would our sports stars be thanked for their decade of service if we couldn't hand over enormous paintings of them, the worst blemishes covered with neatly printed statistics? What would CEOs put in their boardrooms if they couldn't pay tens of thousands for paintings of Allan Donald in his delivery stride? True, his leg seems to coming out of his ribcage, and his nose is disturbingly large, and the left ear seems to be considerably lower than the right, and glue-sniffers have a better sense of perspective, but hell, that's lovely calligraphy on his stats, down there next to his left foot. Wait, shouldn't that be his right foot?

Our unwitting Picassos have been in clover since they discovered that a good photograph increases exponentially in value if you copy it very badly onto canvas. Even now they ponder the technical nuances of their craft in anticipation of

2010: is Ronaldo yellow or brown or sort of apricot-coloured?

Thankfully, commercial success hasn't translated into loftier aspirations, and to date most of their effluent is safely quarantined in log bars and boardrooms away from sensitive viewers.

But what if the pull of the Venice Biennale or the Tate Modern becomes too strong to resist? What would feature in a catalogue of conceptual sports art, apart from videos of a snoozing David Beckham?

Stinky would present a pair of sweat-stained underpants, allegedly worn by Ayrton Senna for two consecutive Grands Prix, daubed with motor-oil, as a representation of Occidentalism in a post-lubricant Latin American milieu.

The controversial *Descent from the Cross* shows an effigy of a naked John McEnroe being cradled by a virginal Tatum O'Neal. A looped recording of McEnroe screaming 'You cannot be serious!' critiques the state of contemporary art discourse.

Naturally the piece by Australian bad boy Burt McWurter entitled *Up Bradman's Bum* would dominate the media coverage of the show, simply because of its scale and iconoclasm. A huge Perspex box filled with 1000 kg of wallaby droppings pillories the Australian failure fetish triggered by Sir Donald's failure to average 100 in Test cricket. Critics point out that 1000 kg is 98.42 per cent of a ton, while Bradman got to within 0.06, but McWurter is too busy setting fire to his hotel room to comment.

The scope is immense: Oxford rowing teams killed and displayed in formaldehyde, a scratch-and-sniff display of old rugby socks, a hole in a wall representing the blurred distinction between the watcher and the watched.

And when it gets out of hand, there's always petrol and matches.

Burning ambition

This raised the ire of a few Rastas. At least I think it did: it was hard to tell if it was ire or just indigestion. Aside: if you have engaged a Rasta in chitchat and realise that he's been talking about Haile Selassie while you've been talking about Heidi and Lassie, walk away without letting on you thought his religion is based on Afrikaans children's television from the early 1980s.

'Dreadlocks are very clean,' said Bunny, shimmering with filth.

His stench formed a tangible brown aura, a pulsating cocoon of throat-clutching pong that orbiting flies either bounced off or burned up in. His pants crackled when he moved, starched with the satanic mayonnaise that drips off the cellar walls of French penal colonies. Majestic herds of lice grazed on the Serengeti of his chest-hair.

He introduced himself and told me he was a Rastafarian. I told him that I was astounded, that I had assumed he was a barrister.

Rastafarians like to be called Rastafari. This inability to remember the fifth syllable is the result of a medical condition called 'smoking weed from the time one can inhale'. A die-hard few still cling on in Ethiopi, the Rasta motherland, but sadly their numbers are dwindling in Lithuani and Nicaragu.

On the whole Rastafari are unflappable. Drive over their shins in downtown Cape Town and they shrug, seeing the bone fragments in your Pirellis as the specks of humanity in the great wheel of Jah's love. Set fire to their hair, and they will admire the Catharine-wheel effect of hundreds of burning fleas jumping clear. In fact, unless one is proposing to outlaw pre-pubescent ordeal-by-dope initiation ceremonies, it is difficult to rouse them to any kind of excitement at all.

But this weekend the Olympic Torch is in Cape Town, and if anything will get Bunny hopping it is the sight of what seems to be a huge smouldering silver bong coming his way, held aloft by a posse of upstanding citizens.

This is by far the most famous faggot to pass through the city, and all the stops have being pulled out. Last week Sarel van Deventer, the city's representative for the Delft Local Organisation Committee, revealed to SAPA that 'the Delft community, specifically schools and community organisations', would embark on a Clean-Up Campaign along the torch's route.

Heads are certain to roll in the Cape Town sanitation department. Why, Director Blikkies Rommel wants to know, have we not been using schoolchildren for years? You can pay them in Marie biscuits and they'll go into tricky little places that regular sanitation workers won't, like gutters and parks.

Delft is rightly named after its Netherlandic forebear. Both are perennially soggy, the inhabitants facing submersion every time it drizzles. Both huddle against freezing winds blowing straight off an icecap. If the flame of international fair play still gutters dimly after Delft, its further survival should be a doddle. Unless someone drops it overboard en route to Robben Island.

In fact a carefully timed fumble by the starboard railing, ten minutes out of port, might be a good idea for those who don't want to have to figure out how to look dignified and sombre while succumbing to meths fumes and toxic smoke in a tiny airless cell.

Somehow I managed to miss the process of deciding which worthies were going to hike through the muddy polders of Delft and all the rest. If he'd been conscious, Bunny would almost certainly have voted for Haile Selassie, Supreme Emperor of Ethiopia and the World (in fact, ruler of everything not already governed by Field Marshal and King of Scotland, Idi Amin).

I don't know who has been ordained to accept the flame on behalf of Cape Town and South Africa, but it isn't cartoonist Zapiro. Perhaps the Greeks are still sore about his 2000 cartoon in which a bergie spoke for the nation, hissing 'Athens se ma se p**s!'over a papsak. The frame, and the way it was clutched to the bosom of the people, neatly demonstrated that the country was in no state emotionally or intellectually to host anything more than a baby shower. But journalism, like love, means never having to say you're sorry.

In the end it should be a stately affair. Dignitaries under umbrellas, ankle-deep in last week's sports section and unsold peaches (where are those damned Delft kids when you need them?), will huddle over the Olympic Cauldron, warming themselves with Zippo lighters as they wait. Bunny will rouse himself from slumber under a wheelbarrow to ask what gives.

Zapiro has a deadline, and so no one is there to yell out 'Athens se ma se p**s!' as the flame arrives, although Bunny gives a fine rendition of 'Buffalo Soldier'.

The rain is heavier now, and in the cauldron the cubes of Blitz have started floating.

The Other Evil Empire

Golf spelt backwards is flog, which is what I did to the joke about method acting below. To within an inch of its life. Still, it was nowhere near as obvious and patronising as Hollywood is whenever it decides to save the world one photo opportunity at a time.

Laurence Fishburne is considered one of the finest actors of his generation. His generation includes Sylvester Stallone.

Those who are doing the considering, usually chat-room visitors called 'Viking Wolf' or 'Soul Thresher' (16-year-old mounds of asthmatic nearsighted acne), say that Larry is one of the last true method actors. And they seem to have a point.

For his role as a dope-addled teen in *Apocalypse Now*, he became a dope-addled teen. For the deep-space chiller *Event Horizon* he was spaced out and deeply chilled. In space no one can hear you yawn. However, his greatest triumph was as Morpheus in the *Matrix* series, a role that combined perfectly the barbiturate quality of his character's name with the Goth-dork angst of the whole ghastly thing. His soliloquies, apparently written in fishfinger on an Etch-a-Sketch, galvanised the youth to go out and buy the tie-in merchandising and to feel superior and dangerous while doing so.

But Fishburne is not only a pretty face, and this week he was in South Africa, revolutionising our thinking. It turns out that child abuse is a bad thing. I found this jolly helpful, and wrote it down for future reference.

Larry is also very pleased that the South African media is

portraying the youth in such a good light. None of the local editors who in later interviews referred to him, mantra-like, as 'Laurencefishburne' were up to suggesting that if his own portrayals are any indication, adults are manically depressed intellectual poseurs who solve conflicts with long bursts of machine-gun fire and judo-chops to the throat.

What next would he say? Global warming is warming the globe? Breastfeeding mothers shouldn't inhale nerve gas? But as quickly as he had arrived, he was gone.

It's just as well he didn't stick around long enough to catch the latest instalment of the trial of Peter Marais and David Malatsi, accused of wanting their palms greased in return for greenlighting a golf estate in Plettenberg Bay.

If he had, he would no doubt have pointed out that golf estates are estates where golf is played. But you don't need to be a finger-on-the-pulse crusader like Larry to know that golf is a major worry to those concerned with global security.

According to *Scientific American*'s website, golf courses cover a chunk of our planet equal to the area of Hawaii, or a third of Belgium. Which begs the question: what's happened to all those Hawaiians and Belgians, torn away from their luaus and chocolate fondues, babies screaming, grass skirts catching fire and seventeenth-century china crockery shattering under storm troopers' boots as they're herded into trucks and disposed of?

They are a forgotten people, these golf refugees, gaunt figures flitting through the dusk along the world's fairways, furtively digging up sand traps in search of ancestral cufflinks. But the human tragedy of golf is dwarfed by the environmental and military consequences of its quest for lebensraum.

An average golf course needs about 3000 cubic metres of water per day, which is as much rain as Botswana got in the nineteenth century, before the drought set in, and not all Middle Eastern sheikhdoms are demure enough to paint their dunes green. Israel is already keeping a sharp eye on the condition of Egyptian and Syrian fairways. After all, one hot summer of typically profligate irrigation by its neighbours could escalate the security situation from the current Code Lush Green to Code Brittle Yellow or even Code Dusty Brown, which would see the Zionist Entity invaded from the north and south by brigades of water tankers and swarms of holy warriors carrying buckets.

Realistically, though, a Golf War seems unlikely, given American military golfing expansion. Despite plaintive cries by American taxpayers, the US armed forces maintain 246 golf courses around the world, three of them at Andrews air force base. Given the American military's motto ('If it's ain't broke, break it and buy a new one') one can only imagine the diesel-evaporating Humvee golf carts, the razor wire and searchlights on every out-of-bounds area, the machine guns and concrete in the bunkers.

And if you think they're going to let some five-putting, sweet-spot-enlarging, shorts-wearing, par-three-playing, handicap-fudging Commie camel-jockey use American water – sweet, icy Montana stream water, bathed in by beavers and pretty Navaho girls with big brown eyes – to irrigate your degenerate undemocratic nine-hole mashie courses, then you're about to get your priorities rearranged, son.

Larry Fishburne would want us to crack the carbon-fibre shank of neocolonialism on the knee of free will, and to toss the ball of oppression into the water hazard of enlightenment. Otherwise …

Today, Plettenberg Bay. Tomorrow, the world …

Ag shame

Readers will be pleased to learn that since this column appeared in June of 2004, Mr Bojangles has been appointed in a senior management position in South African rugby, and Mrs Bojangles is no longer on antidepressants.

There is no torment of regret so fierce, no prostration abject enough, to compare with those the moral columnist must undergo when he sees that his work has done cruelty to an entirely innocent party. Callous and cavalier, he has broken a true and honest heart, a heart that knew only love and hope before his cyanide paragraphs killed forever that irreplaceable spark of joy.

It was the least I could do – for yes, amazed reader, I am the ghoulish bounder who has done this irreversible mischief – to visit the victim of my thoughtlessness at her home, a modest concrete enclosure decorated with some straw and a tyre on a rope. Mrs Bojangles was not at home, so I left my card and retreated. I have not heard from her since.

However, since then I have received word from those who know the Bojangleses that her condition is morbid. Her plunge from the heady euphoria of believing that her husband was going to be the next Springbok coach (a fiction invented in this column five months ago) to the horror of learning that it had all been a crude literary device, cheap laughs stolen at the expense of her dreams, has been more than her little three-foot frame can take. Worst of all, she had already paid the deposit on a new tyre for the baby's hutch, and had to face the humiliation of returning it and some bananas she had bought on credit.

Three Tests into Jake White's tenure as coach, it is clear that opportunities for chimps are now pitifully few. Gone are those heady days of Rudi Straeuli when, hindsight now suggests to us, entire troops of primates were recruited to handle tactics, team morale, media liaison and public relations.

But perhaps I have toyed enough with the emotions of chimps and should say no more on the matter. The reality is that one could probably prove in court that Straeuli's entire coaching team was human, given DNA-samples and the testimony of priests who baptised them and didn't remember more than the usual covering of hair on the infants' backs.

So, given this revelation and the grace and effervescence of White's team, the question begs to be asked: what on earth was Straeuli doing for all that time? Sawing at players' Achilles tendons to toughen them up? Telling them that tries were for sissies?

Rudolf is gone with Prancer and Dancer and Staaldraad and all his other assistants, but the mysterious Danish rot still lingers, if a *Weekend Argus* columnist is to be believed.

It seems that the recent scrapping of contracts is upsetting the ickle snookums ruggy-kicky players. Where once they could wander off towards the bench, gatvol and overweight, and still get a seven-digit cheque at the end of the year, now the poor devils have to stand cap in hand for one-off appearance fees.

In line with this new exploitative system, Springboks who play all the Tests in an average year – 12 or 13 – stand to make between R900 000 and R1.2 million. But it gets more shameful.

In tones usually reserved for discoveries of bootlegged porn DVDs in scoutmasters' trunks, the piece reveals that because of his injury woes Ashwin Willemse is staring at the horrifying possibility of pocketing just R300 000 over the next twelve months.

'Does SARFU really value our top rugby players?' bellowed a front-page tagline. Clearly this was intended as a sort of Wasp '*Amandla!* ' requiring an '*Ngawetu!*' about how poorly our lads are paid in comparison to, er, other rich people.

But somehow it all seems a little obscene when one looks over to the constable sitting in the dead-ball zone in a gentle drizzle of naartjie peels, on a blessed sabbatical from gunfights and exponentially multiplying case dockets, who takes home about R3000 per month. That's what our hard-done-by Springboks are likely to earn in a day. Any day. Every day. A Sunday by the pool. A slow round of golf, a leisurely braai.

Of course the industry will insist that players' earning life is short. The implication of this line – that these boys are uneducated, unskilled, and unprepared for real life – never seems to be recognised by those who recite it.

It's a hard life, they insist, with real sacrifices. No. Being a policeman is hard. Being Mrs Bojangles is hard. Earning 95 times the national per capita income for playing a game is not hard.

In the meantime: flowers and a written apology, or just bananas and a beach ball? Now *this* is hard.

Hellish Hellas

Timeo Danaos et dona ferentes. Look it up and quote it to your Athenian waiter down at the Taverna next time he brings you the kebabs he's just assembled after unblocking the drain in the kitchen. It's Latin, so he'll smile and nod uncomprehendingly, and you'll feel superior for a day or two until you go down with salmonella.

For too long science has overlooked the hillbilly. Perhaps fearing being tied to a tree and molested, anthropologists and sociologists have eschewed the deep woods, failing to draw back the mosquito net of secrecy that still obscures this remarkable tribe.

Scratch the surface of the hillbilly, and we find little rolls of dirt and traces of antifreeze under our fingernails. Wash the surface and then scratch, and we find the story of humanity itself.

Hillbillies know nothing of borders or of stifling modernity. They know nothing of anonymous urban sprawl. They know nothing of income tax and credit cards. They know nothing of dental hygiene or spelling. They know nothing of their immediate ancestry. But who needs the book-learning and chompers when one's empire extends from the termite-infested porch of this little life to the tree line of eternity? Certainly, the truck-on-bricks of failure, rusting next to the long-drop of disappointment, is a concern to those living the examined hillbilly life; but look away to the sunset, where all the world's treasures flutter on the washing line of opportunity! Life is beautiful.

Until now the history of the hillbilly has been vague, owing to his inability to remember where he was 48 hours ago, but it is a history spanning all times and cultures. San folklore tells of the !Yi-Ha clan (translates roughly as 'marry sister live in hole in the ground'), who would trek for a fortnight across the Karoo to borrow half a calabash of milk for the baby, with promises to pay it back in monthly instalments.

The Sioux tolerated the shaman trances of the notorious slacker Squats With Beavers, stuffing wampum in their ears as he plucked at a ukulele with his one good tooth; medieval Holland was a reluctant home to the Schtoepkakkers of the Schtinkvoet swamps. French hillbillies, called *montguy*, established Gallic sanitary habits that endure today. In Germany they were called Swiss and given their own country in the mountains to the south.

Times have changed, and hillbillies are losing their heritage. George W Bush and Michael Moore, hellbent on proving each other to be white trash, simply have no way of knowing that they are in fact distant cousins, illegitimate great-grandsons of the Reverend Cletus Gomorrah Chewknuckle of Anus County, West Virginia.

But then, in one flyblown corner of the world, hillbillies flourish in virgin squalor: Greece. It takes an extraordinary race of no-accounts to invent Western civilisation and, four thousand years later, have only some kebabs to show for it: this is backwoodsy sloth at its most undiluted, a failure of ambition of epic dimensions. Athens is anthropological gold-dust.

Anglo-American antiquity-worshippers have prettied up their history and culture, but some stains run too deep. Who else but hillbillies would wage war naked, or go home from discussions on the planets to an underage male concubine?

You can call ouzo whatever you want, but moonshine is moonshine. And as for bouzouki music, two words: banjos, *Deliverance*.

Given all of this, last weekend's news from Athens should not have surprised one. According to *The Telegraph*, the Olympic committee (pop, mom, brother-dad and sister-aunt) have decided to poison the city's 15 000 stray dogs, because 'the sight of packs of dogs roaming the streets will harm Greece's image'.

Call me elitist, but any city stalked by packs of strays has bigger worries than its image. Like the safety of its pensioners and toddlers, for starters. Ari, won't you be a dear and nip across to make sure old Mrs Nikolaides hasn't been dragged out of her wheelchair again and isn't being eaten under a bridge?

The article didn't name specific breeds, so we might be talking about 15 000 feral Maltese poodles, ripping out the throat of anyone who tries to shift them off a comfy lap. But once a mountain-man decides to poison something, be it a raccoon or a New York property developer or his own liver, there's no stopping him, and the dogs of Athens are doomed.

Those entrusted with Greece's image have surely considered the prospect of thousands of dogs scattering into subways and unfinished stadiums to choke to death on their own blood. Perhaps it is an image that evokes in them some kind of nostalgia. You can take the hillbilly out of the backwoods, but you can't take the backwoods out of the hillbilly.

And in the next weeks, as the Olympic city lays out lethal treats, Athenian dogs will come to fear the Greeks, even when they bring gifts.

One Day in the Life of
Ivan Tennisovich

Anyone for socialist intercourt ballistic détente?

Here she is, this Nabokovian sun-child, crystal-cold Russian tanned to honey by a decade in the heat of American skin-worship, giggling as she lifts her trophy. Ten thousand Humbert Humberts, comparing over-earnest notes on her forehand, look at the girlish knees, the still-soft calves, hair the colour of a Ukrainian wheat field, and endure the delicious torment of being old and ugly in the shadows as this new love-liness dawns over the tennis world.

Of course that's not the version the women's game and the protectors of womanhood would like one to notice, and certainly Maria Sharapova's nerveless performance on Centre Court elevated her at once from pin-up to official Wimbledon highlight, a teenaged winner with a goofiness in her gracious-ness to match Steffi Graf or Boris Becker or all those other spotty and precocious champions who have come before.

But one can't blame the Humberts for their undiscerning adoration, because greater forces than even Serena Williams's neckline are at work here. Perhaps it was the Soviet Union's last great subterfuge. Perhaps the West's decadence has result-ed in a failure of comprehension. But somewhere in the last ten years a new and entirely false factoid was grafted onto the Western male consciousness. From men's magazines to the lascivious covers of *Cosmopolitan*, the new order was declared: Russian girls are hot.

Of course, it was just the hair. It was Churchill who first pointed out the immense pull that Russian hair exerted on the Western imagination, declaring the country to be a riddle wrapped in a scrunchie inside a bottle of conditioner.

Anna Kournikova, the original Miami Menshevik with a spring in her steppe, was the prime example of the hallucinogenic qualities of blonde locks. Put a paper bag over her hair, and one finds a nose like a blob of play-dough squashed between little piggy eyes, and pork-chop cheeks subsiding towards a mouth of supreme churlishness.

In fact, Kournikova's is the kind of face that should be covered in tractor grease on some far-flung collective farm. It is the face of the Motherland, pretty as a potato and sensitive as a steel mill.

Which causes one to digress: why did tennis take so long to take hold in Russia? In 1990 there were an estimated 200 tennis courts in the whole of the Soviet Union. At 10 000 kilometres from west to east, one had to sled 50 km at a time to get a game. Those who missed the court by a degree or two north or south would have stumbled on into the snow for weeks, finally eating the dogs and burning their tog bags, their white shorts and shirts making them invisible to rescuers.

Certainly Stalinist sports lovers would have found in tennis a microcosm of everything they were ordered, on pain of death, to hold dear. Equally matched rivals faced off across a rope curtain. The launch of a small Sputnik-like orb set the enemy scurrying, and the ensuing strategic positioning of ballistic objects compelled both parties to scramble into the far corners of their respective empires to ensure the status quo. Tramlines, baseline, Cuba, all had to be patrolled.

Meanwhile there was the economy to worry about. Scoring was achieved through limited production linked to enormous inflation: one point scored counted 15. But wealth foments capitalist perversions, and when workers acquired 30 points their earning capability was handicapped by the lone dictator who presided over the match. The next point earned just 10, and the next – the winning point – was an undisclosed number. Did one need 41 points to win? No one knew: such finite targets were bad for morale, and prevented defections to the West where once could earn 50, 60, even 80 points a year on lush grass courts.

But nothing was perfect except Stalin, and sometimes one's opponent managed to muster 40 points too, usually thanks to the conspiracy of international Jewry, satanic Catholicism and the CIA. This score, known as Deuce in the West and as Détente in Russia, was a transitory peace, a patently obvious smokescreen behind which the forces of aggression were mobilising. Naturally this situation requires a pre-emptive strike to gain the Advantage. A kick-serve up the middle, or a veto, usually did the job.

And now Russians are free. Free to be poor, free to be blown up by terrorists or Mafia crime lords or leaking gas pipes, free to be alcoholics in the privacy of their own dumpsters. Free to move to Miami when they're five. Free to win Wimbledon.

I love a happy ending.

Turn again, Muammar …

His rich; he's had Lockerbie removed from his rap-sheet by greasing Western palms; he plans to be President of Africa; but the Libyan despot is still unhappy. Yep, there's just not enough conditioner in the world for hair like that.

Last Saturday *The Guardian* reported that a Mr Muammar Gaddafi of Tripoli had expressed an interest in buying an English football team, specifically Crystal Palace. By Monday, as both the club and his aides denied the rumours, he had subsided into a deep gloom.

'Viceroy,' said his Grand Vizier, 'the error was not yours.'

'It said "crystal palace" in the classifieds,' said Gaddafi, peevishly ruminating on a prune. 'Not Crystal Palace.'

'It did, Brigadier-General. Both the Calligrapher Laureate and Optometrist Royal have confirmed it.'

'And if I told you I wanted to buy a crystal palace, would you assume I wanted some English soccer team staffed with Nubians and financed by Jews?'

'Never, Air Marshal!'

'Wouldn't you assume, as a logical man, that I wished to acquire a palace consisting largely of crystal?'

'Always, Grand Dragon!'

'Exactly. Why do the English vex me so? This prune has lost its flavour. Bring me some Quality Streets. Just the green ones. With coconut inside. If I find a praline I'm going to have you castrated.'

The Court Projectionist cleared his throat and bowed. 'Wing Commander, today I will be showing *Harry Potter and the Prisoner of Azkaban*. It is the story of an English boy who ...'

A great roar echoed through the pink quartz corridors, startling the Peacock of State into flight. 'Torment me not with pubescent English shamans! Put on *Dirty Dancing* again. Fast forward to the bit where Patrick Swayze sings "She's Like the Wind." That's a good bit.'

He slumped onto a pouf, a present from Robert Mugabe, who was busily purging all poufs from Zimbabwe. He looked longingly at his empty appointment book.

'Perhaps I should buy Crystal Palace after all,' he said. "Look what happened to Mohammed Al-Fayed after he bought Harrods. They think he's Winston Shakespeare over there. Ali G interviewed him. Why hasn't Ali G interviewed me? Is it because I am African?'

But no, he knew, that wasn't it. It was so unfair. The English liked you or they didn't. The English and all their stupid little customs: the poached-eggs-before-wicket, banging sausages and mashed potato chips in newspaper, stiff upper chin, their stupid flag that they copied from those novelty underpants you could buy in Carnaby Street. And yet there was something about Hyde Park in summer ...

'You're a man, aren't you?' he asked the Grand Vizier.

'Thanks to your continued saintly restraint, Holiness.'

'Well then, tell me what a man like Tony Blair is thinking. I called him – I know, I know, you're not supposed to, but he wasn't going to make the first move – and it was lovely. How's the weather, how's the tent, how's Cherie, how are the court whippets, that sort of thing. And then he asks me about

Lockerbie. I mean, why not just ask if I've got herpes?'

'The English are barbaric, Excellency.'

'Verily. So speak: am I back in favour, enshrined once again in the mildewed English heart, or do I have to send flowers and small cash settlements? They say flowers say it best. I still think napalm and nerve gas say it best. Oh, it's all so tricky! Maybe I should buy Manchester United also. And Wales. They say it looks a bit like Chad, but not quite so pretty in the spring. Perhaps a crystal palace in Wales. I could turn the first sod, and abolish the pound. We could call it the Islamic Welsh Emirate.'

'They will make you Lord Mayor of London-town,' said the Grand Vizier. '"Turn again, Muammar, thrice Mayor of London-town." It was Puss in Boots who said that. Al-Fayed will be sick with envy. You could ban the Harrods sale and outlaw Liberty print fabric. You will be invited for dinner with David and Viqtorya Al-Beqam.'

'Get me the number of the Crystal Palace Football Club!' cried Gaddafi, too excited to notice that he had eaten a praline. 'And Andrew Lloyd Webber: two million pounds, opera, me, horses. Scarlett Johansson to star. Hugh Jackman to play me.'

'But what about Lockerbie, Effervescence?' asked the Grand Vizier.

'What about it? Those Scots love their football. I'll buy that famous Scottish team – Celery Sticks. No, the other one. Hibernation. That's it. You'll see. Give them a smile and a football game, they'll forgive most things.

'Besides, people forget everything in the end. Now pass me the remote. Oprah's on in five minutes.'

Dear Martin ...

*'Two! Three! Four! Five! The lights are all on! And it's ...
No! No! No!'*

For almost a decade, as Murray Walker indulged his dangerous liaisons with English idiom, Martin Brundle was the forgotten man of the ITV Formula One commentary box. The
eternal butler to the devilish seducer of mixed metaphors, the
former racer swept up the split infinitives and polished the
spoonerisms as Walker plunged ever deeper into linguistic
notoriety and the hearts of his audience.

There were those who resented Brundle's move behind a
microphone that for years had been the undisputed domain of
the honey-voiced James Hunt, one of those rare Englishmen
who, like Roger Moore, possess diction so perfect and inflection so assured that it seems a shame they don't spend their
days disarming nuclear bombs while reciting the St Crispin's
Day speech from *Henry V* before taking 22-year-old physicists
called Inga into uncharted realms of carnal bliss.

That was an appallingly long sentence, blistered with osten-
tation and hyperbole, and frankly the sort of thing Hunt
would never allow. With such large velvet slippers to fill,
Brundle was always up against it. And it didn't help that he
brought to the job the plaintive, receding inflection of a mis-
firing biplane wobbling across a cornfield before subsiding
into a distant copse of trees.

But our Martin knows his stuff. By modern standards the

racers he drove in the early 1990s look like Russian knock-offs of Chinese copies of Klingon battle cruisers on bricks, but the difference between hitting a wall in 1992 at 250 kph and hitting a wall in 2004 at 300 kph is academic. More than that, he's one of the only people in the world who almost beat Michael Schumacher in a Grand Prix once.

The retirement of Murray Walker saw the superfluous James Allen paroled from the pits and installed in the number two seat, with a mandate to froth. Suddenly Brundle's contribution has gone from interesting to invaluable: his understated techno-lingo, his gently cavalier attitude to sudden, public death on the racetrack, the whole package now seems the only thing between Formula One for the aficionado and the great nodding, gushing, gasping, speculating mass of fans who populate the stands and press boxes of the world.

It was worrying, therefore, to witness at last weekend's German Grand Prix a disturbing hint of transparency creeping into his commentary, an unpleasant eagerness to explain the sport to newcomers.

According to SuperSport, 'the more you know, the better it gets.' I assume this excludes elucidating photographs taken by a private investigator of one's wife and her masseur. Or the knowledge of what seagull bones and feathers do to a Boeing 747's engines as you settle into your final approach into Honolulu International.

Televised coaching has its merits, certainly. It takes extraordinary restraint to watch Ian Botham demonstrate the correct grip for an inswinger on Channel Four and not send down an over of short-of-a-length naartjies at the water cooler. But Formula One?

'For those watching, that's the perfect way to take the inside line,' said Brundle on Sunday. 'He stays aggressive and gets on the gas early. Brilliant.' Brilliant indeed, but for whom? A hitherto unknown legion of amateur grand prix drivers, taking notes off their televisions? Did retired matrons hiss 'I *told* you that was the perfect way to take the inside line!' and slap their sheepish spouses with a rolled-up Michelin catalogue?

Has Formula One gone cricket? Has ITV started down the donnish path that ends in Test Match Special, with monologues on the merits of Windsor knots? When will Brundle start reading out letters on air?

'Mildred from Romford has sent us a lovely cake – it's a hit with the Ferrari pit crew, there's marzipan all over the fuel hose down there – and she writes as follows: "My husband Wilfred turned 70 this year, and we all chipped in to buy him the 2001 Arrows car, with a rebuilt Mugen engine. Every afternoon after his nap he takes it out onto the R34. Unfortunately he has found that on 200 mph inside-outside bends he tends to black out. What can we do? Is it the nap? He is also a little overweight."

'Well, Wilfred's problem is a common one, and nothing that hasn't happened to all of us at one time or another. Mildred, tell Wilfred to pick earlier braking points. That should clear it right up.

'Now here's one from Klaus of Stuttgart. "Hello Martin, how are you being? *Alles kla?*" Thanks, Klaus, yes, *alles* is *kla* and thanks for writing ...'

Lowering your sites

You know it was a slow week when the media starts watching the media, and columnists have to subsist on other people's headlines.

When International Olympic Committee president Jacques Rogge walks into a room and introduces himself, people instantly spring into action. This is because they think he's choking to death on a herring bone. But apart from having a glottal seizure for a surname, he is by most accounts a fairly popular fellow.

So when a Malaysian news site ran a story on Tuesday entitled 'IOC's Rogge Sleeping with the Athletes', it didn't seem entirely outlandish to speculate that a hands-on managerial approach was being implemented in the Olympic Village: a romantic candlelit tryst over a plate of protein slabs, husky innuendoes exchanged between sips of decaffeinated isotonic rainwater; the awkward question of whether or not to use performance-enhancing drugs; and finally, as the moon set over Athens, cries of 'Citius! Altius! Fortius!'

Somewhat disappointingly it turned out that Rogge was merely slumming it in the Village in something the Greek media were calling 'Spartan' accommodation. The sleeping, one must therefore assume, happens on a bed of thorns from which he is woken by means of a brisk beating by a naked man wielding a plank with a nail through it.

It was a valuable caution to those of us who, too well informed and busy to do any actual reading, glean our weltanschauung from website headlines. Indeed, such insight would have been a welcome antidote to a disturbing report of supernatural Oriental pandemonium, appearing a day earlier.

'Chinese Fans Go on the Rampage', read the headline. One shuddered, imagining the horror of being trapped in a Beijing alley by a rogue swarm of paper fans, their leader menacingly furling and unfurling to reveal a stylised painting of a sinister duck on a nest; the terror as its minions flap at one's face, clogging eyes and throat with faintly salty rice-paper; a hinge-pinch on an ankle, the first bead of blood, an unholy rustling; darkness …

It was a relief, then, to learn that Chinese football supporters had been throwing things at Japanese fans, and that Sino-Japanese relations in general were quickly heading in the direction of oil embargoes, gunboats and other reassuringly normal diplomatic high jinks.

But it's not easy to clamber back onto the wagon of literacy once you've fallen off into cyber-superficiality. Especially when faced with headlines like 'Willie Becomes 19th Tiger to Qualify for Olympic Games', which appeared on Monday. Was Willie's late inclusion a tacit admission of an under-strength team in the Muddy Watering-Hole Synchronised Splashing event? Or could we look forward to Willie anchoring the 4 x 100 Punjabi Villager Chase-and-Eat Relay?

Alas, no. Willie is Kelly Willie, a student at Louisiana State University (whose mascot is the tiger, because of all the tigers that live in the bayou) who has joined the American relay squad. Boring.

Of course one wouldn't indulge in headline-extrapolation if most of them weren't self-explanatory; and they don't get much plainer than 'Pakistan's Only Female Athlete Has

Humble Ambitions', posted on the website of the Saudi-based *Arab News*.

As South Africa observed Women's Day, Sumera Zahoor told AFP that she has come to terms with the impossibility of winning a medal in the 1500-metre event, and now wants only to finish ahead of last place to save herself from shame. Go get 'em, wildcat.

One can't blame her, though. Already considered a feminist paramilitary cadre for running in poly-shorts rather than donning traditional black mosquito-netting, Ms Zahoor's best chance of settling ruffled patriarchal feathers is to reassess her humble ambitions, perhaps exchanging her second-last place for a healthy boy-child, which would be far more useful to everyone.

Still, Sumera's obstacles seem slight next to the pressures bearing down on Rubab Reza, Pakistan's other only female athlete. (Perhaps swimmers don't count as athletes. Perhaps swimmers don't count as people, what with all that shameful nakedness, all that tossing of long black hair.) Sixteen-year-old Reza is keen and pragmatic yet slightly apologetic, no doubt realising that she will be dragging herself into the wakes of better swimmers through a volume of water that could irrigate her country for five years.

But one wonders how much of her the folks back home will see. Turn it off, Cousin Mahmood! Haven't you read? The IOC president is sleeping with the athletes! He was a sailor, for Belgium. The worst kind. Look at the poor child, shivering in the shallow end. And don't they know there are tigers about? They swim, those tigers. O child, come home! Come home and find a husband!

Strong fences make good
neighbours angry

*When athletes indulge in acts of political defiance at the Olympics,
the world takes notice. Heaven knows why. After all, these are
people who left school when they turned nine, and whose contribution to society will end when they turn 25 or twist their ankle,
whichever comes first.*

Australian daytime television tells us that everybody needs
good neighbours. Naai-burrs, goes the ditty, Ivry-bawdy nades
good naaaaaiii-burrs. And they're right. Who wouldn't want
to live just a blackjack-infested lawn and splintering picket
fence away from Kylie Minogue? Granted, she was still just
Leedle Coily back in her soap days, and not yet an interna-
tionally famous rabbit-toothed bottom, but still.

Unfortunately good neighbours are hard to find. Of course
there are sporadic reports of people who have managed to
move in next door to an ivy-covered abbey whose inhabitants
have taken a vow of silence, and whose devotions manifest in
the compulsive baking and distribution of chocolate cake. But
most of us must face a reality of Great Danes barking like
howitzers, pre-dawn weed-eating extravaganzas and pre-teen
shrieking competitions.

To be fair, they're not oblivious, these neighbours. Often
they pop a note through the letter box – 'Hi mandi and sandi
are having there 10th birthday pordy tonight and there will be
shrieking from about 7pm until Thursday thanks mandi and

sandi's mom tandi' – and Tandi has gone to great pains to explain why the howitzer barks.

'He barks when he's scared.' So far it appears that he is afraid of postmen, pedestrians, his kennel, the affections of his owners, daylight, moonlight, and wind.

Pity the Greeks, then, having to live next door to the Middle East. For five thousand years they've tended their shabby-genteel home as it is gradually overrun with honeysuckle, ruminating every few years that they should sort out their television reception and do something about the moles blistering the lawn. And every weekend for those five thousand years they've considered phoning the police about the racket coming from the rusted shack and adjoining flyblown outhouse next door.

Of course, long ago they used to visit, and that nice Israelite, that Paul fellow, used to send postcards quite a lot; but his correspondence tailed off about two thousand years ago, and after-dinner chats about philosophy soon became strained when it transpired that the Middle Easterners had only ever known and practised one philosophy: tribal self-righteousness backed up by killing, which was known as 'smiting'.

So imagine the agonies of embarrassment, the long-suppressed blanches at past faux pas, when Iranian judo champion Arash Miresmaeili refused to fight an Israeli opponent in Athens last week.

Most hosts would have welcomed such pacifism – judo in the living room invariably ends in recriminations about broken vases – but to the Athenians, and indeed the rest of the Olympic village, this was par for the course from the malcontent goatherds next door.

Iran, you see, doesn't recognise Israel's right to exist, and bans its citizens from any contact with Israelis. It also doesn't recognise very much after the fifteenth century, but that's another story. Miresmaeili is now the golden boy of the Iranian revolution, having stuffed his face with kebabs to be overweight at the weigh-in and thus be disqualified. Somehow acts of conscience don't seem quite as impressive when the defiant one has gravy trickling down his chin, and has, through sustained gluttony, compelled an administrative body to effect his protest for him.

But Iranian president Mohammad Khatami is tickled pink. Miresmaeili, he told the Islamic Republic News Agency, is a hero whose protest 'will be recorded in the history of Iranian glories', a history that will now extend to almost two sides of a sheet of foolscap.

Of course, there's a difference between being a dope like Miresmaeili and his president, and doping. In fact the only possible explanation for why the Greeks didn't tell the lardy judoka to pack up and get on the next bus to Tehran is that they are busily refraining from throwing stones. After all, they've been polishing the glass house for eight years.

And it takes time to create a masterpiece of watertight fiction like that offered as an explanation for Kostas Kenteris and Katerina Thanou missing a doping test. The couple, it seems, were speeding along on a motorbike, a Balkan James Dean with his Doris Day clutching tight, when they were pranged, probably by a Turkish Cypriot terrorist. Then a Samaritan arrived and drove them eighteen miles to hospital, where they lay in untested splendour.

So far the Grecian fuzz haven't been able to find the wreck, the Samaritan or, most crucially, witnesses. And as the pair watch the Games from sidelines, they must be ruing that missing ingredient. Where's a nosy neighbour, peering over a picket fence, when you need one?

What I think

What I think, with hindsight, is that a lot of people can't spot irony even when it's being ladled to them in bucketfuls: my inbox floundered under a torrent of e-mail from people agreeing with everything I said in this piece and desperate for a kindred soul with whom to share their prejudices. I stopped replying, and started investigating emigration ...

I think therefore I am, said Socrates, and he was right. Obviously times have changed, and today's thinkers, people like Gene Roddenberry and Gnome Chomsky, are more insightful on the whole, but Socrates' motto is still worth celebrating, as our capacity to think is what separates us from the animals.

Not that animals don't think. I am certain that dolphins feel love, especially for the handicapped, and they've proved that monkeys can be taught to speak, if you wire them up just right and stimulate certain pain centres. I've seen footage of a rhesus monkey saying 'Oo ee aw ogh oo ee!' which was quite clearly the start of Hamlet's solenoid from the play called *Hamlet*.

But on the whole I am proud of my God-given ability to think, the product of a million years of evolution. I don't want to sound vain, but I think a great deal, about many things.

For example, I think that Princess Diana of Wales was a candle in the wind. I think she did more for humanity than anyone in history. I think Madiba probably did almost as much, but he was fighting apartheid (which died anyway when he was released), and also they've proved that Africans don't have a genetic understanding of democracy and non-violence, so he was probably frustrated by having his good work undermined by that.

The candle in the wind and Madiba are my heroes because they didn't hate anyone. Of course there are some things they did hate, like tyranny and paparazzi photographers and apartheid and the Queen, but these are good things to hate. I think everyone should have good things to hate, which means they should hate bad things.

Me personally, myself, I hate people who make generalisations about foreign cultures. That's why I hate the English: Brits are always making sweeping statements about everyone. And the Afrikaners – I really hate them. Not the ones you meet, the ones with educations and a sense of humour, I mean the other ones. Stupid crunchies with their sideburns and their religion.

Not that I think religion is bad: I think one should try to embrace as many different faiths as possible, to give one a balanced view of spirituality and God. Except for Islam, which they've proved is based on violence. And Judaism, of course, which isn't really so much a religion as a lifestyle. A bit like Buddhism, really: anyone can join as long as you have all the accessories, like that little book the Jews tie to their heads. Which reminds me, I think that set of miniaturised classics they've just brought out looks absolutely stunning.

And speaking of Afrikaners, I think all those crunchie dentists who've taken the chicken run to London are unpatriotic racist cowards. They've refused to see the good in South Africa, like the Springboks and Cyril Ramaphosa and the

Waterfront in Cape Town, and they dwell on the bad, like the way blacks are genetically inclined to corruption.

Obviously living in a democracy means we're entitled to live wherever we want, and my neighbour is moving to Toronto, because of the affirmative action. It's getting so bad that he's going to have to downsize to a Volvo before he leaves. But I think that living in a democracy also means you have a responsibility to support that democracy, even if you haven't voted for it, or it doesn't necessarily give you proportional representation. And that means supporting its sports teams also.

I don't believe in pointing fingers, but Trevor Manuel is setting a very bad democratic example by supporting the All Blacks and not the Springboks. I know he's switched sides now, but that also doesn't set a very good democratic example. (They've proved that he's Portuguese and I don't need to tell you about the Portuguese.)

But what I've really been thinking about a lot lately, what's been burning me up, is how much I hate Clyde Rathbone, that lily-livered chicken-running pseudo-Australian. I think South Africans take sport far too seriously, and so everyone is missing the point about Rathbone: it's not that he isn't playing for the Springboks that's so offensive. It's that he is a repulsive traitor, who should have got his face smashed in at Kings Park last weekend.

And did you see how reluctantly he shook hands with the Springboks afterwards? Precious fairy. Some people just don't understand sportsmanship, that's what I think.

Arry Stotle and Philosophers Moan

... but emigration would have meant having to tidy my flat, so instead I just wrote a column about it.

Professor Bruce of the Philosophy Department at the University of Wallamalloo (Queensland), most famous for his theories on the drinking habits of Aristotle, would have succinctly described conditions in Athens last weekend, as the Games came to close: 'It's hot enough to boil a monkey's bum.'

However, after the events of this week, I must hasten to point out that Prof Bruce (along with colleagues Bruce, Bruce, Bruce, and Michael) is a fiction, co-authored by Cleese, Palin et al. and published by Python, Monty, some forty years ago. There is no evidence to suggest that Aristotle was a bugger for the bottle or that René Descartes was a boozy fart. In fact, although it was very hot in Athens last week, it is probable that most monkeys attending the Games came away with scalded, rather than boiled, bums.

Not that any South Africans would have been able to keep an eye on those simmering simians: they were all too busy phoning me.

Readers of this column might recall that last week's offering began by mistakenly attributing Descartes' 'I think therefore I am' to Socrates. It then went on to make a great many further mistakes. To explain them – which I have been doing all week – is to re-enter the nightmare world of German joke-telling: ze following choke is full of humour. Vonce I heff finished telling it, I vill explain it to you point by point …

Suffice it to say, a great many readers of this newspaper know their Greeks from their Frenchmen (which is more than Chinese gymnastics judges can manage, handing out a 6.3 to anything not in a red leotard). Most of those who called or e-mailed were jovial and slightly ashamed of their erudition. But some seemed genuinely disturbed.

One professor of philosophy (a real one, whose university shall go unnamed) told me that he regularly urged his students to read my column, and that they would now be misinformed. One was tempted to suggest that if his students are getting their education from the sports pages of newspapers, they've got bigger problems than misattributions; but so earnest was his concern, so laborious his delivery, and so profound his failure to grasp irony, that an apology was hastily issued before the temptation to scream hysterically into the phone became too great to resist.

I should have been reassured by the outpouring of feedback: any society so well versed in Cartesian sound-bytes can only be of sound mind. But as the e-mails and telephone calls stacked up, disturbing questions began to surface.

Why, in this charitable tutorial, was no one pointing out the dwarfish deviance of Gnome Chomsky's new name? Why had I not been made to suffer the slings and arrows of outraged unfortunates over Hamlet's 'solenoid'? And most disconcertingly, if these readers considered the column an honest if bombastic declaration, why was I being allowed to saunter away, like Br'er Rabbit from a briar patch, after an outpouring of racist vitriol that would make a Grand Dragon blush?

To escape the Greeks, the French, the lingering doubt that

the volume of comments indicated a failure of the writer's rather than his readers, I sought solace elsewhere, and, like so many other refugees from the cultural maelstroms of Europe, I found it by a televised pond somewhere in the American south-east.

God bless America, and I don't mean that facetiously. As the world's broadcasters scrambled for space in the smoky Olympic stadium and the closing ceremony degenerated into Greek Eurovision song contest auditions, as millions of people craned for one last flicker of the muted rush that has been these Games, a regional bird-dog championship wound gently to climax.

It was a tranquil pronouncement of independence and the rights of the individual, in this case the right to guide a fat Labrador through reeds in pursuit of a rubber duck. As Nike swooped back to Olympus, Nike the bitch was having trouble spotting the last decoy, and her owner was fretting in the meadow above.

Finally, with disappointment no less intense than that of an athlete tripping on a hurdle, the man resigned himself to what the commentators called a 'vocal go-around' and the dog sheepishly found its quarry. The man soothed her and played with her ears, but Nike couldn't bring herself to look at anything other than her wet paws.

Looking at this calm, ignored corner of the world, one couldn't help wondering what Descartes would have thought: I think differently, therefore I am?

Crips are winning the turf war

Hell hath no fury like the lobby for the disabled. This column unleashed a deluge of complaint from people who thought I was mocking the chair-bound. Still, at least I got to make the acquaintance of the head of the body that deals with doping, who wrote to me and the paper declaring this to be the epitome of poor taste and, just to make it stick, called me a racist because I'd suggested elsewhere in the paper that more blacks need to be selected for the national cricket team. Sticks and stones may break my bones …

Try to remember the kind of September when grass was green and corn was yellow. Or, if yours was an upbringing blessedly free of musicals, try to remember being little enough to have had an eternally stubbed toe and only scabby brake-pads for knees. Try to remember having jam on your forehead and burrs in your hair.

Now remember sitting on the sandpit wall, sucking processed cheese out of your cardigan as you observe, with what will one day become morbid ennui, a brutish 7-year-old beat a tiny girl on the head with his lunchbox. Remember your detached horror as he makes for you. Recall the outrage as the lunchbox crashes down upon your own burr-crowned head, reeking of fermented orange juice.

And then the final shock: being told by Teacher not to fight, monkey-boy, and your sweet, innocent self being handed identical punishments, being told that it's not important who started it, that you're both being wicked. Remember when you first realised that aggression is never punished, that innocence is ignored, and that people who espouse tolerance and inclusiveness are uptight passive-aggressive sociopathic frigid vegetarian Nazi hippies.

But an uptight passive-aggressive sociopathic frigid vegetarian Nazi hippy's gotta make a living, and so most of them have left education and gone into the world of lucrative indolence known as 'marketing'. And the most zealous egalitarians amongst them are currently selling us the Paralympics.

Celebrate the triumph of the human spirit, they urge. Ignore the clank of titanium knees and the ponderous swimming races and our own instinctive (and confusingly insensitive) pity for beautiful, magisterial bodies broken or truncated. Look past the blunt unheroic opinions of the owners of those bodies, people whose lives have been focused as much by necessity as by a competitive drive. Look past it all, because sport makes us all equals! Well, okay, we make a heap more money than you, but marketing salaries are market-related, so really that's not our fault. We're all equals in spirit, and that's what counts. Except for conservatives. They're pig-dogs.

But the trouble is that triumphs of the human spirit aren't generally open to the public. In fact usually only one or two human spirits are involved, and they're too exhausted to do much celebrating, whether they're on the summit of Everest or on a deserted bus homeward bound from a night shift at a factory. And in sport you can't sell discipline and control and fiercely private triumphs over fiercely personal demons.

The reality, despite the rhetoric of equality, is that there is no vicarious pleasure in disabled sport, except for those families and friends who have borne a portion of the histories and exceptional efforts involved. We are simply not that evolved, and nor should we be: that much empathy can only lead to migraines, dizziness and death.

Which is why we need an Olympic tournament for athletes afflicted with disabilities simultaneously sensational and banal, where champions can carry our dreams in their clammy hands, our hopes in their fibrillating hearts. In short, games that recognise that most sport isn't a celebration of the human spirit but a polite wait for bloodletting.

Just imagine the riveting spectacle of the final kilometre of the Consumptive Marathon, the effete field of writers and painters dabbing at the corners of their mouths with silk handkerchiefs. Consider the dramatic value inherent in the Leprosy Hammer-Throw, where it is common for contenders to give their left arm for an extra few yards of distance.

True, events like the Ebola Steeplechase might tax more sensitive constitutions, but for those willing to put aside their squeamishness, sporting intrigue abounds: is that a water hazard or the Honduran contestant? When the Congolese runner collapses on lap four, should one take out a stretcher or a hosepipe?

Eczema beach-volleyball would be slow and irritating for players and spectators alike, but there's always osteoporosis judo, by all accounts a cracking sport. And aesthetes could hold their collective breath as little Lala Vcsvrcsu of Romania swerves wildly to port on the beam in the Inner-Ear Infection gymnastics discipline, her life unwittingly saved as an errant .22 slug from the nearby Hay-Fever Pistol-Shooting Range skims by and ricochets off the gelled coif of the Ukrainian judge.

Motion-Sickness Yachting, Gout-and-Jerk Powerlifting, Epileptic Table-Tennis: the voyeuristic hypochondriac would be spoiled for choice. In this turf war the Crips have already staked their claim. It's time for the Bloods to do the same.

A full quota of African democrats

All those in favour say 'Zzzzzz …'

So splendid was the agenda, and so eloquently was it read, and so warm where the sunbeams streamed down through the stained-glass representation of the ascension of Idi Amin, that the delegates at the first sitting of the Pan-African Parliament decided to adjourn for half an hour to indulge their democratic ecstasies.

As they licked the goose-liver pâté off Salticrax in the banquet area their murmurs were unanimous: there had never been a more democratic agenda in the history of democracy. The will of the people had been heeded. The people didn't want to talk about Zimbabwe, and presto! Zimbabwe was not on the agenda. The people found it tiresome to talk about the Great Lakes region and Darfur, and just like that, in an orgasm of democratic excellence, they too had disappeared from the discussion table.

In fact, as Gertrude Mongella, the president and speaker of the gathering, settled herself behind a tray of sausage rolls, she realised that every single person in the room was a democrat, in some way or another. Last weekend she had been challenged by an undemocratic newspaper about the efficacy of a parliament intended to foster democracy comprising many non-democratic countries, and she'd run rings round their reactionary pseudo-logic.

'We are at different levels of democracy,' she'd said, and as she reached for the mustard she congratulated herself on the clarity of her democratic vision. What the naïve reactionaries would never understand was that almost all countries were democracies. The feudal dictatorships of the United States and Great Britain liked wagging fingers at North Korea and Saudi Arabia, but the democratic facts remained: there is no poverty in Saudi Arabia; homosexuality has been eradicated with tremendous success; nowhere are woman safer than in the tight embrace of their husbands. In fact Saudi women don't even have to work or go to school. As for North Korea, was it afflicted with racism? Bourgeois materialism? Surely any country in which food shortages affected all equally, and no one had more political rights than anyone else (including farm animals and tree stumps), was evidence of the flourishing of multi-levelled democracy?

Her reveries were interrupted by the popping of the official champagne cork signalling the next session. Already the ushers were gently frisking the Senegalese group, notorious for smuggling out crème brûlée under their fezzes, and the delegation from Chad had accelerated their efforts at the meatball table, stuffing their jacket pockets with reckless zeal.

When they took their seats, accompanied by the unmistakable sound of pilfered lasagne being sat upon, it emerged that the first order of business – a discussion over the appropriateness of spelling 'Africa' with a 'c' rather than the more ethnic 'k' – had been bumped in favour of a snap debate over racial quotas in sport, chaired by the ANC Youth League.

The League's credentials as chair were unquestionable and its impartiality legendary: its openness to democratic adaptation had been underlined by its insistence on quotas – to the point of threatening boycotts – and, eighteen months later, its declaration that quotas were unworkable and unsatisfactory.

'What is sport?' whispered the leader of the Mauritanian delegation. 'I have not heard of this.'

'You know,' muttered his Sudanese counterpart. 'Shooting at black women and children from the back of Isuzu pickups, that sort of thing. Sport.'

'And why would you need racial quotas?' asked the Mauritanian.

'It is more democratic that way.'

In a makeshift tent of jackets propped up with rulers the Zimbabwean delegation was desperately trying to get clear reception on the earpieces issued by Jonathan Moyo's Information Ministry. At last the static cleared, and the tent was collapsed with a flourish. The Zimbabwean chairman raised his hand. Harare wished to speak.

'Why is there still debate about efficacy of racial quotas in sport? Surely —' The chairman poked at his eardrum and flinched as a flock of pigeons a thousand miles away raised hell with the signal; but quickly his feed resumed. 'Surely any right-thinking person has to see what a perversion of democracy they are; how they obstruct the processes of ensuring that African democracies henceforth field only black players? The Zimbabwean cricket team has proved the no no dammit I ordered a blonde girl, not this cow, get her out of here. The Zimbabwean cricket team oh for the love of God can't anyone organise a decent hooker any more?'

There was a smattering of applause, and then they adjourned for lunch.

Stoute Kabouter versus the Black Knight

This one is dedicated to all those children who, like me, thought for a time that there was nothing more rare and wonderful than witnessing Wielie Walie's little bee – Bytjie, I believe – playing his trumpet to summon Bennie Boekwurm (who, it must be said, looked ominously like the late Dr Allan Hendrickse).

They call me Liewe Heksie, but Lavinia is my name. I'm the cleverest witch that I know, and I've even been to the moon. That's how I used to say hello to the children. It used to rhyme, too, when the nice uncles at the SAUK let me do my show in Afrikaans. That's all gone now. I'm not complaining, though, you understand: my new place is small and the roof leaks, but I have my health, and they're almost sure my pension has been delayed by an administrative error, and not something bad.

Yesterday I was in Blommeland and Blommie bought me a cappuccino and we were talking about the old days, before the children got so sophisticated, before they started saying terrible things about King Rosencrantz, things about his – that he was – that he was a girly-man. Then Blommie says to me, 'O Heksie' (he still uses an Afrikaans 'o', which doesn't have an 'h' after it and sounds much more fatalistic), 'O Heksie,' he says, 'have you seen this kak list of kamma Great South Africans?'

'Haai-o, Blommie,' I said, '*dis nie mooi nie.*' I hate it when Blommie uses swearwords, because whenever a kabouter says something ugly it makes a flower die. When they cancelled our show and took the straw out of Sarel Seemonster and Karel Kraai over on the *Wielie Walie* set to use in bricks for RDP houses, Blommie locked himself in his car with a case of schnapps, and half an hour later the windows were steamed up and all the flowers in Namaqualand were dead. (Bennie Boekwurm, you'll remember, got an anonymous tip-off and went underground before the vans arrived, but they say he's got emphysema and someone stepped on his glasses so now he spends his days alone, crying in the dark.)

Yes, it's not nice to say unkind things about people, and when people say unkind things to me it makes my heart very sore. I don't talk a lot because Blommie says if you don't know much about something, don't say anything about it, and I don't know much of anything. But *heerlikheid, mense*, if a white-bread mullet in a puffer jacket and platform tackies like Steve Hofmeyr can get in ahead of Oom Sisulu and Oubaas Mbeki, then paint me black, give me a *pielietjie* and call me Tokolosh, because we've got our priorities *opgevoeter*.

A whole lot of flowers started dying when Blommie got onto talking about Jeremy Mansfield, but I told him he was being very unfair. 'Blommie,' I said, 'Oom Mansfield entertains a great many people.'

'So does Mandrax and hookers,' said Blommie, and King Rosencrantz's prize pansy turned black and fell over. 'And they're the same demographic.'

Blommie is just sore about this because Athol Fugard is his idol, and Oom Athol came in stone last, about fifty spots behind Oom Mansfield. 'Blommie,' I said, 'you know as well as I do that given the choice between *Boesman and Lena* and *100 Kak Jokes That Will Make Your Poephol Sting*, most people will opt for the poephol. *Skuus dat ek so vloek.*'

'Speaking of which,' said Blommie, 'I see we almost had a cheating thieving perjurer in the top ten.' I said I thought Winnie Mandela *was* in the top ten, and Blommie went very white. '*Jirre, bokdrolbrein*, you can't say stuff like that! I meant Hansie Cronje.'

'At least there are a couple of worthy sporting heroes on the list, like Naas Botha.'

'No, he's not.'

'Well, like Graeme Pollock then.'

'No.'

'Basil D'Oliveira? Jake Tuli? Ezekiel "King Kong" Dlamini?'

'No. But Gary Player's in the top ten.' Blommie teed off at a tulip with a length of hosepipe. 'If you think about it, he's the perfect guy to represent the last three hundred years of South African sports, a rich white man strolling about on a mani-cured lawn, with skinny cattle staring longingly at the back nine rough, his heart firmly in the right place and his golf bag firmly in the hands of a klonkie. I suppose the idea is if he's handing you a 9-iron, he can't put a burning tyre around your neck.'

'Sies, Blommie,' I cried. 'Your cynicism goes too far! Oom Player is the Black Knight! Oom Player gives money to poor people!'

Then he said I was bitter because I wasn't on the list and Eugene Terre'Blanche was, and I turned him into a goitre, and now we're not speaking.

Willows in the Wind

The clever men at Oxford
Know all that there is to be knowed,
But they none of them know one half as much
As intelligent Mr Toad!

The dam in question is brown and long, squeezed in as an affront by water nymphs between desiccated farmlands and the ruddy oven walls of the Cedarberg mountains to the east. Last weekend it was three-quarters full, but the sun-crushed bluegums on the waterline haven't been dampened in years, and the grass, optimistically spreading across the mud flats, is already yellowing. The white sky and ticking, desperate rocks of January are coming.

But at least for now the dam has a domesticated air about it. The breeze in the afternoons is pleasant, not yet the blowtorch of Christmas, and the geese in the shade of the willows fuss and flirt with gusto. It is a scene that you might consider photographing, if the camera wasn't packed so deep in your bag, and if it wasn't so damned hot. Next time.

And so the dams of South Africa pass by, with their weaver nests and their disconsolate gangs of rehydrating sheep, their surfaces sometimes stirred by hot gusts, their perimeters patrolled by rusted barbed wire, here and there an optimistic sign declaring the privacy of property and threatening legal action against the children of farm labourers who trespass like gleaming naked otters among the reeds.

Pass by, that is, until one finds a boat; because boats change everything about dams. Water Rat from *The Wind in the Willows* spoke true when he declared that there is nothing – absolutely nothing – half so much worth doing as simply messing about in boats. Which is just as well, since most who get their lubberly hands on boat, on a weekend sojourn at a distant dam, are unfit for anything more than simply messing about.

Each grind of oar in rowlock, every foundering averted by wild bailing, confirms Ratty's assertion. One has never truly known happiness until one has stuffed the prow of one's boat into a mud bank, out of sight of civilisation, and got free again by gyrating back and forth while pushing wildly at said mud bank with an oar. This is freedom.

And then comes the slap of a little ripple amidships, and another, and you look up from the cans floating about around your feet and the mating dragonflies on your shin, to see a wake intersecting with your plotted course; and over yonder, like some sort of piratical tennis shoe crammed with gadflies in bikinis, a motorboat fishtails its monogrammed rear all over the tranquillity.

Suddenly the jetty looks terribly far away. The laughs of the gadflies and the virile belching of the tennis shoe seem to mock these honest efforts, these splintering timbers that even now are insinuating themselves into your underwear. The breeze has come up, and along with it the sobering realisation that you are being pushed crabwise towards something that is either a tractor tyre or an anaconda.

Back on shore with hands cramped into blistered claws, the joyful musings of Water Rat seem terribly naïve. What this lark needs is engines, one decides, great big things fed on terribly expensive fuel. And suddenly another character in that novel begins to materialise by the water's edge, one with a cigar in his thin green lips and a mad twinkle in his bulbous eye.

The speed-crazed Mr Toad was, you will remember, an incorrigible hedonist, a fallen amphibian brought low by his fetish for automobiles and the hellish delights that they provided in the region of 40 miles per hour, and by his penchant for grand theft auto. Indeed, his final reformation and transformation into a toad of substance was at the expense of those leaden-footed ecstasies of velocity. But oh, one now wonders, what would Mr Toad have made of these sleek white launches that torment the lay rower?

Would he, as I did, suddenly understand the lustre of water sport? Would he gaze entranced at the little throttle lever, enticingly topped with a Red Button? What would that Red Button do if pushed? Light afterburners? Launch photon torpedoes? Would he too stroke the little plastic bucket seats, noticing the intriguing way some of them faced backwards, as if their occupants had been unnerved by rushing towards destiny like a stone skipped across a pond? Would he catch himself murmuring 'Nyeeeooowrrrr!' as he fingered the steering wheel?

A rush of blood, a choked cry, a splashing lunge, a splutter of engines! On, you beast! On! Ownership and tomorrow be damned! Fly! Run! Roar! Nyeeeooowrrrr!

Six degrees of suppuration

A member of a certain party's Youth League e-mailed me after this one appeared and said he had been deeply disturbed by what seemed to be my implication that universities should be elite institutions. As a graduate, he wrote, he found it offensive to the fight for equality in education, and when I'd figured out his spelling ('graduet', 'ofansiv', 'equalty') I offered a polite and non-committal reply. Of course I should have quoted Mr Incredible to him: if everyone's super, then nobody is …

Communist, Afrikaner, author of *Dracula*: Bram Fischer was many things to many people. Christened Brambleberry Foxglove Fischer, he rejected his bourgeois roots in the 1920s and briefly changed his name to Bram Tractor Fish-Packer after a visit to the Soviet Union. On his return to South Africa, flush with the royalties from *Dracula*, he committed himself to a life at the bar, but the last round had already been called and his life at the bar lasted just another ten minutes. He subsequently dedicated himself to a life outside the bar but was asked by the local constabulary to move along.

Or something along those lines. That's the trouble with dying in the dark, two decades before the shutters were opened in the 1990s: Fischer missed out on canonisation for want of a decent publicist. Like an inconvenient face in an old politburo photograph, Fischer's likeness in our national portrait has disappeared under the clever fingers of ideological retouch artists.

That is, it had until this week when a postgraduate at the

University of Stellenbosch suggested that he be awarded an honorary degree. Alumni dug their heels into the fertile, pap-sak-strewn soil of that fair borough, and threatened to blockade the Stellenbosch Farmers' Winery with a ring of S-class Mercs.

Which seems fairly uncharitable, given the university's long history of offering recognition to outright basket cases. Observe the Maties rugby club, the biggest in the world with an estimated eighty teams: surely any institution that happily sends alumni magazines and college ties to people who sat on the reserve bench for the Maties 78ths can include one yellowing political memory?

But perhaps that's just the point: had Fischer punted the pigskin for a team with only mild disabilities, say the rickets-racked 42nds, he would no doubt have stood a far better chance of academic promotion. Indeed the front page of the university's website this week suggested that Stellenbosch is actively breeding a new kind of achiever: 'Flute-Playing Swimmer Excels for SA in Tunisia' read the headline, further evidence of an academic programme intent on splicing sport and culture.

The curious reader was entranced. Had her fingering and mouth position been crisp enough to prevent massive consumption of seawater during her oceanic recital? Had wholesale pandemonium broken out amongst sonar operators in passing submarines? Disappointingly it turned out the alumna, a flautist when not swimming, had merely become the first person in the world to swim round Africa's most northerly point, which Dutch immigration officers insist is Rotterdam but which is actually somewhere in Tunisia.

No doubt she will be awarded an honorary Doctorate of Music and Oceanography next year; and why not when University County Cork gave James Bond actor Pierce

Brosnan an honorary gong earlier this year, the same Pierce Brosnan who left school at fifteen?

But at least Brosnan is reportedly charming and sophisticated, which is more than can be said about many of the sportsmen now crowding graduation podiums around the world. Manchester United's Roy Keanne, another Cork graduate laureate, knows many things: how to extract maximum pain per pound of force exerted on the human shin; how to look hard done by at all times; how to express his world view in just two syllables. But with all due respect to Dr Keanne (DPhil Head-Butting), he probably thinks 'cum laude' is an instruction from a porn director.

Still, at least acceptance speeches are short. In July this year the Italian football referee Pierluigi Collina was made a Doctor of Science by Hull University for his services to sport. You know, because of all the science. Winning everlasting adoration with his oratory ('Hull seems like a nice city'), he went on to marvel at the curious events going on around him.

'It's not usual for anyone to receive an honorary degree from a university,' he said. Luckily for his self-esteem the Sultan of Brunei wasn't also on the podium, awaiting his 133rd degree.

But in the end one can't scoff at the players. They're just pitching up for the free sherry. It is the universities – many of them little more than activity centres for naked wealthy orang-utans – which devalue degrees. Central Ohio State University probably has at least one functionally literate lecturer on its books, but it all crystallises when visitors trail their fingers up the maple-veneer honours boards, past the names of pork-product tycoons and bipolar televangelists, to 1989.

Because that was the year COSU awarded a Doctorate in Human Letters to Mike Tyson.

Number one with a bullet

An AK–47 bullet weighs 9.6 grams. This means that whenever someone in the Middle East is buried, or every time someone in the Middle East is having a party, or every time someone in the Middle East stubs his toe, our planet is briefly lighter by around 12 000 kilograms.

> Kurds do it, Maccabees do it
> Particularly angry Lebanese do it
> Let's do, let's shoot in the air.
> In Spain secessionist sets do it
> Osama's troglodyte cadets do it
> Let's do it, let's shoot in the air.
> The folks in old Palestine do it
> Not to mention the Tamils
> Saudi sheikhs supine do it
> Though it frightens their camels.
> Egyptians for a lark do it
> Protesters in Hyde Park do it
> Let's do it, let's shoot in the air.

One would have thought that any society au fait with the physics of suicide-bombing would have figured it out long ago: what goes up must come down. Certainly, unshakeable faith in divine providence goes a long way, but prefacing every prediction with 'God willing' tends to deny certain realities about the effects on cranial bone of rapidly falling AK-47 bullets. Being faithful is one thing. Being a blithering idiot is quite another.

And idiots there were aplenty in Ramallah this week, as the helicopter bearing Yasser Arafat's body descended over his compound into a hail of hysterically aimed small-arms fire. If God's will was being imposed anywhere over that dusty armpit of the globe, it was all focused on that terribly brave pilot.

So why do these ballistically challenged young men insist on unloading their Kalashnikovs into the sky? Sociologists have been unforthcoming so far, perhaps because their research budgets don't extend to hardy flak-jackets and helmets; but it seems that an entirely new form of human expression is developing.

So far socio-linguists seem to agree that 100 rounds from an AK-47 aimed at 85 degrees express abject grief, while 150 rounds from an Uzi directed at the vertical indicate joy. This will have been a great consolation to the families of the scores of Kuwaitis shot to pieces after the liberation of their country by the Americans in 1990: the Kuwaiti army, realising it couldn't very well go through an entire war without firing a single shot, threw itself and its stockpiles of ammunition into celebrating the victory.

But there are more questions than answers. If dad lets rip with his Glock at the ceiling of the lounge, is he celebrating the outcome of a dog race or asking the missis to bring him another grape juice? If she rolls a phosphorous grenade back through the door, is she reaffirming her love for him, or hinting that it's time to re-upholster the settee?

What a relief to live in the West, where assault rifles are used only for hunting salmon. How gratifying to have ardent defenders of intellectual independence like Michael Moore and John

Pilger telling us what to think. But most of all, how pleasant to be able to watch sport and not fear random death from above.

And the Irish fans, packed parka to parka in the hypo-thermic stands at Lansdowne Road on Saturday, clearly appreciated all those liberties as they cheered and stamped and whooped at the drama unfolding below them. Old men declared they had never seen the like of it in forty years. Children hid behind their father's trouser-legs and gaped. But the footage from Dublin was indisputable: it was a real sun-beam.

About four metres wide, it lay across the try line for at least fifteen minutes, nine minutes longer than the last recorded sunbeam, spotted in Belfast in the summer of 1934.

But ninety minutes of prostrate ball-grubbing later, such sen-timental pleasures were in tatters, at least for South Africans, the sunbeam gone the same way as Springbok delusions of grandeur. With two minutes on the clock, and the deficit five points, even the robotic Hugh Bladen had ceased the curious and utterly pointless incantation of players' surnames that he seems compelled to perform in lieu of actual commentary.

A sudden penalty awarded to the visitors. All eyes on the far touchline, willing a one-metre flag-raising. Bladen re-inflating his vocal bagpipes for one final drone. And then Kobus Wiese saying, 'So, You, does Juan Smit kick for touch or go for the posts?' and silence falling as the virgin imbecility sinks home. The seconds crashing by like plummeting chandeliers, and the growing certainty that Bladen is about to go Tora-Bora, drilling Wiese stone dead, high-arc trajectories be damned.

But in the end all is clapping and shaken hands and thumped backs. Over Dublin, rounds of applause. Very far away, applauding rounds resound …

Branded for life

The last time I spoke to Justin Nurse, he was buying a one-way ticket to South America. Something about tequila rather than beer being the drink of choice in rural Ecuador.

I drink Diet Coke. It makes me feel good. It helps me retain my boyish figure. It calms me down. It peps me up. It sings me to sleep at night. I love Diet Coke. I want Diet Coke. I need Diet Coke.

Advertising people will say this is because of branding. Branding, you will recall, is what happens when you've told a lie for so long that you start believing it yourself. Because of branding, they will insist, Diet Coke is my friend and confidant: I was taught to love Diet Coke by clever executives.

Which is nonsense. I love Diet Coke because of something called phenylalanine, a highly addictive chemical with cell-retarding properties. It's so bad they have to mark it on the can with an asterisk. If you feed it to babies you will produce junky vegetables. My brain and mouth tell me that Diet Coke tastes like the run-off from a communal shower in a Cairo brothel, but my heart whispers sweet, phenylalanine-fuelled nothings …

Of course you can't always drug your clientele, and so branding seems the next best thing when it comes to suppressing those emotions that prevent us from swimming with piranhas or buying German sedans on credit. South African Breweries, currently shacking up with fellow booze-pimp

Miller, seemed to have got branding down to a fine art. Until Justin Nurse and Laugh It Off.

Those who were raised not to stare at ugly people might not know that SAB Miller last week recommenced its systematic flaying of the incorrigible brand-defacers. It was all so terribly confusing. Why, if the corporation is concerned about its brand, did it do absolutely nothing when the cricketers it sponsored were found to be cheats and hypocrites, or the coach of the rugby team it backed was fired for being a racist, or the same team became synonymous with footballing idiocy?

It could have been worse. It often is, when money and sport mix. Certainly it was a touch shortsighted to keep Hansie Cronje's five-storey visage looming over Newlands for six months after he was rusticated. But perhaps they didn't have any ladders handy to get up onto the wall of the breweries and scrape Cronje into the dustbin of ignominy, being too busy peering over Justin Nurse's wall.

The Gestapo treatment being handed to Nurse's enterprise is repugnant, but it is not a moral catastrophe. Big sharks eat little fish. Schoolyard bullies kick chubby 6-year-old girls in the shin and grow up to be CEOs with anorexic trophy wives. And so the world turns. But one can't help thinking that there must be some terribly stupid people sitting in some terribly expensive offices, because this is what the SAB Miller brand now tells me:

(1) There is no threat too small to squash, which means they're worried about their brands, which means there might be something wrong with their brands, which is as good as saying they're mixing anthrax with urine and putting it in cans.

(2) Castle Lager and Black Label sue fun people.

(3) Castle Lager and Black Label don't have a sense of humour.

(4) Maybe it's time for me to start drinking vodka. And watching the cricket from home. Fully clothed. With my bags packed and my visas in order.

But most importantly SAB Miller has told me that it is desperately, toe-curlingly, nose-pickingly uncool. In the space of a year they have gone from patriotic cheerleaders and roistering purveyors of bonhomie to faceless slabs of grasping corporate grease, their post-nasal drips plopping onto their patent-leather shoes as they struggle to get their bicycle clips on.

Indeed, suddenly their terribly stupid television advertisement for Castle takes on a wicked subtext. South Africans, blessed with superhuman strength apparently gained from mainlining jingoism, drag the world's great landmarks towards our own shores. Before they began beating Nurse with bags of oranges (still the simplest way to break bones and rupture organs without causing bruising to disturb spectators), that advertisement merely stank of a curious nouveau-colonialism and arrogance fuelled by ignorance.

Now we have to ask ourselves: if a Buckingham Palace guardsman refuses to be towed south by SAB Miller, will they sue him? If we point out that the anchorman in this enormous tug-of-war is black, and if we suggest that he is doing most of the tugging, will we be subpoenaed for raising the spectre of black labour?

I love Coke Light and I'm scared of SAB Miller. And that's branding.

Cringe in a bush

Cousin Evelyn's dialect confused some readers. Cawnt firthlay-fivmeh imedgin whey: sparfectlair cleah. Isn't it?

The conversation had turned towards the literary potential of the Garden Route, but despite the Major's staccato insistences that he had once skimmed a slim volume about a resourceful prostitute with a wooden leg living in Knysna, it was agreed that nothing readable had ever been set in the bosky territory that lay beyond the polo field.

Arabella Slenter-Flay clutched the linen of the tablecloth and tried to become invisible. Any second now they would smell her dirty secret, the stinking degenerate Dutch abomination that crouched, rolling its *r*'s and tugging at its khaki socks, in her brain. It would be like Daddy in the mines, when the blackies would try to smuggle out diamonds up their bottoms and Daddy would say 'Where d'ya think you're off to, Othello?' and send Matron for the rubber gloves.

For the truth that dare not speak its name was that Arabella Slenter-Flay could speak Afrikaans. Worse than that, she could read it, and had done so, once. Something called *Kringe in 'n Bos*, about elephants and coloureds. Her ears burned, and she was certain that soon a huge festering red 'A' would rise up on her forehead, her shame branded there for all to see. She remembered last year's regatta, when handsome young John Brewins was revealed as Jan Bruins, son of a dentist with a possible history of Judaism; the thunderous seconds in which it was unclear whether his fiancée, Daphne Organza-Garter, was going to use her brand-new shotgun on him or herself. In the end she used it on his Landrover, but the legend of the Flying Dutchman, born as Jan fled into the Tsitsikamma Forest, lingered on.

'Bugger me, not a book!' said the Major. 'A real gal. Just remembered. Plunged her for a fortnight in '38. Damn spirited. Wooden leg gave me concussion. Let her wash my shirts. Sweet thing. Should have married her.'

Dear, sweet Major! The bookish talk passed, and she reflected on her close shave. She remembered Great-Great-Granddaddy's similar escape at Isandlwana, when he had shown the famous Slenter initiative by strapping a Welshman to his front and a Scot to his back, and hiding under a heap of dead Irish.

It was quite beautiful, this country, when you thought about it. It could obviously do with more water features, and President Umbeeky would have to address the plague of Port Jackson bush sooner or later, but when you looked at it in a certain way, it was almost as pretty as Virginia or Provence in early spring. The comforting whine of chainsaws came to them on the breeze from across the river, where another polo ground was being cut out of the blighted woods, and down in the estuary the little black shapes of bulldozers scooted this way and that like happy beavers, levelling a new golf estate. It was progress, and progress made her happy.

Progress also made her Uncle Leslie happy. Somewhere around that headland, he too was transforming a muddy, stinky wetland into a pristine estate where dozens of people could enjoy nature on beautiful green lawns, and come to know the majesty of Africa in conservatories full of stuffed leopards and buffaloes. Of course, progress didn't come cheap, but Uncle Leslie had always known the right people, and what was an undeclared Mercedes or three next to the eternal rewards of nature?

The third chukka was just starting when Cousin Evelyn, who had set off southward in search of a golf course, returned. He was a sweet boy, despite an eternally over-wet bottom lip, and it seemed he was enjoying his South African sojourn, away from the pressures of looking out of the window of his father's London bank. If only they could understand what he was saying.

'Gort teautly lorst,' he said, collapsing into a deck chair, and everyone nodded and smiled. 'Peskair wode-sains all in Afwicorns. Rate, wortivay missed?'

'Must be a bit thick to miss a golf course in these parts,' said the Major. 'Neither fish nor fowl, eh?' He winked enormously. 'In-breeding. Horrible thing. Never crossed my mind. Had an absolute knockout of a sister once. Thighs like a gelding. Never touched her, though. Pity.'

A loerie skimmed out of the trees and made for the east paddock. This was the essence of sport, Arabella thought, to be outdoors under the sun, with good friends.

She got off both barrels at the bird but missed.

Home movies

A very bad idea ...

Why people should be so disturbed by public displays of affection is beyond me. Surely it is only the morbidly cynical and the adolescently insecure who fidget at the sight of two young things sitting on a park bench admiring their own reflections in each other's eyes. Indeed, few pleasures can be more gentle or affirming to those of advancing years than watching the courting rituals of the young, perhaps through a pair of non-reflecting binoculars from the tranquillity of a public toilet, or maybe from a fourth-floor window with the benefit of a telescope equipped with night-vision technology.

But Frans Cronje's public announcement, made with genuine tenderness last week, that he was making a film of the life and death of his cricketing brother, was not affirming or inspiring. It was just embarrassing. In families there is always someone on hand to clear their throat loudly to cover for a beloved grandmother's obliviousness to her thunderous flatulence during dinner, but here there was only an awful silence.

In fact it was the awful silence that follows fifteen minutes of the adored son extracting from his violin an impression of cats being spit-roasted alive; of utterly stupid poems droned in broken and halting language, hailed by all as sure signs of genius. It was the appalled lull experienced by the visitor when he realises he is being made complicit in this worship of mediocrity. Either he must stay and surrender to sentimentality, or get his coat and leave. But that would be rude, and besides, the savouries are excellent. And so the observer stays, resenting that he is being used as a cog in another family's rituals, loathing the object of all that affection.

The Cronjes love their lost son. Frans loves his brother. It is entirely understandable that a family would have been 'increasingly frustrated over the past four years by the often inaccurate, out-of-context and one-sided interpretations of Hansie's life', as Frans put it. Again, cringe: the defiance of kin still faithful despite having lapped up one-sided interpretations for the years that Hansie was on the take.

Clearly the family has failed to understand that reputations have nothing to do with accuracy or context or balanced interpretations. No amount of balanced reporting will change the memory of Hansie that is now owned by the public, especially not when the biographer commissioned is called King, and is paid by the Cronjes. The film will preach to the converted in their Grey-Bloem-themed bars in the Free State; and those who despised the greed and hypocrisy of the man will have fresh hate to warm their hands over, as they mutter about Broederbond money and Old Boys' ties and propaganda films.

But the real pillow-biting embarrassment in all of this stems from the earnest, desperately naïve belief of the Cronjes that the South African public will care, that it will actually pay thirty rands to watch the dullest story ever told, and that it will leave the theatre nodding introspectively and not shuddering at the sheer kitsch of it all.

'We feel this is a great South African story with huge worldwide appeal,' said someone excitable at the production company, implying that they reckon there are at least a couple of thousand bucks to squeezed out of it on the straight-tovideo circuit in the United Arab Emirates. But Frans seemed horribly convinced when he said that there were 'many incredible lessons to be learned from Hansie's life, the mistakes that he made and the actions he took to redeem himself.'

This movie sure does sound like a blast. But let's pretend for a moment that the inevitable won't happen, that it's not going to be Disney in the mielie fields, barefoot games of cricket with badly animated singing aardvarks and kudus standing in the slips. Since when were things you mastered in kindergarten, like right and wrong, 'incredible lessons'? And remind me about the part where he redeemed himself to South African cricket?

Frans Cronje should be admired for his loyalty and love, and his decision to act on those qualities; but it is very important for him and his family that this film is never made, that they keep their raw and private totems away from the callousness of the South African public. Hansie is already a national pariah. They don't want him to become a national joke.

The Men Who Would Be King

Is it time for a royal flush in Swaziland and England? And if it is, how big a toilet will they need?

It's good to be the king. Not that Ruddy Prince Harry will ever know. The pink Windsor, his regal epidermis eternally flaking off his sun-blasted ears, has to face a life of listless consumption, an endless round of spending and getting and meeting and forgetting. His eyes, long since bleached from royal blue to the colour of the skies that stretch over desert truck-stops where men in dirty overalls asthmatically stuff the last few femurs of their victims into gym bags, tell us nothing about this bleak future of pointless wealth that stretches before him.

But at least he's in love, according to the Sunday papers. Indeed, like a Zimbabwean canned lion, his princely heart has been tracked by the Selous Scouts of amour, corralled by the helicopters of desire, and blown away by the assault-rifle of infatuation.

The huntress, herself sniped at by telephoto lenses, was declared a 'blonde beauty', the adjective implying the noun to those knee-jerking typists who write such things. But while one is eager to give the benefit of the doubt to somebody who is not only blonde but rich, all yours truly could establish from the grainy pictures (or the parts not obscured by the Giant Red Spot of Harry's noble pate) was some yellowish hair with dark roots showing, and a striking pair of nostrils, reminiscent of a debutante who has run headlong into a plate-glass window.

One hopes they will be happy together in their cocoon of sunscreen and whiteness, but alas, genuine royal excess will forever elude them. They can sizzle on yachts in the Aegean, but they will never match the almost ascetic obscenity achieved by the Swazi monarch this week.

Which is not to say they wouldn't feel right at home. In Swaziland, just as in Sloane Square and Kensington, one in five women are illiterate. Both realms are home to thousands of people who have never had a job. Both have a life expectancy of 39, although, to be fair, Swazis tend to die less from scooter accidents and liposuction complications than of HIV/AIDS and preventable diseases.

So perhaps it wasn't entirely inappropriate for King Mswati the Umpteenth to buy a R3 million car this week, a Maybach fitted with a fridge, surround-sound, and a radar system that locates 16-year-old virgins. Not that there's anywhere to drive in Swaziland: rev and you've hit the border. Still, it's important to show the people – 70 per cent of whom live on under a dollar a day – who's boss.

Perhaps one day Swazis will get tired of living in the thirteenth century. Perhaps one day King Mswati will say 'Let them eat my dust' once too often. Perhaps on that day his subjects will decide to cut their king down to size, perhaps by about a head, with a blunt axe. But until then he provides the region's megalomaniacs and petty godfathers with a role model.

Not that South African football apparatchiks need any encouraging. Having had its lips firmly glued to FIFA's bottom for the last few years, SAFA in the person of its president last weekend detached them with a loud smacking sound and confirmed, with the kind of fart-sniffing armpit-scratching boorishness that has become its stock in trade, that it is drunk on entitlement.

When accused of being an embarrassment by FIFA media committee member Emmanuel Maradas, Molefi Oliphant responded that Maradas had better never set foot in South Africa or he would be 'sorted out by my guys'. Now to me that sounds like the SAFA president kindly offering the services of his personal pedicurist and masseur, but the killjoy Maradas heard a death threat.

Adhering to the principle that if you're going to embarrass your country, do it properly, Sports Minister Makhenkesi Stofile waded in to wag a finger at FIFA's apparent desire to have a say in the appointment of a tournament organiser. 'That is not the right thing in the spirit of democracy and good governance,' he said. While this sentence was not the right thing in the spirit of grammar and articulate speech, it served to remind one that anybody who mentions democracy, good governance and FIFA in the same breath either is desperately stupid or is trying to sell something.

Either way, all concerned were missing the basic point: FIFA needs SAFA like Swaziland needs a Maybach. 2010 might be signed and sealed, but how long until the trophy hunters decide to add an Oliphant head to their wall?

Skop, skiet and soccer

In 2010, as knuckle-duster-wearing Scousers and Rammstein-chanting Berliners trample South Africa under hobnailed boots, perhaps those shrill suburban pastoralists who protest about bent daffodil stalks after every Ajax–Sundowns game will discover just what real football hooligans are, and just how good they've had it …

The Sky News 'Hijack Live' box was disappointingly immobile. As Rupert Murdoch fed the informational equivalent of white sugar to England's lowest common denominator on his news channel, the picture-in-a-window resolutely refused to show anything resembling what broadcasters were calling 'drama'.

After ten minutes a policeman had walked past, and the rolling billboard behind the bus on the dim Athenian street had changed ten times. The camera had wobbled for a moment, caressed by some Olympian zephyr; but of drama there was no sign. Somewhere in dark mahogany offices Sky executives wrestled with the difficult question of what to show should a massacre ensue. After all, how fair to their viewers would it be to keep their Live-Cam pointed at the bus once the shooting started? No doubt this prospect was unanimously rejected. No, the good stuff would have to be filmed close up, preferably with sound, with an artistic emphasis on exit wounds and tear-streaked cheeks. Leave the stodgy fuzzy telephoto rubbish to the dorks at the BBC.

But still nothing happened and Splatter-Cam remained

dormant. And so, perhaps fearing that the natives were becoming restless and might switch over to something more informative (like, say, *Eastenders*), the channel proceeded to run a short film starring George Bush's dog, scripted and edited by somebody lured out of rehab with state-funded crack. The Republican cur was supposedly searching for the new White House puppy: it trotted this way and that, was lectured by an appallingly wooden President about bein' a gurd dowg and not poopin' on the Oval Office desk or humpin' Dick Cheney's leg and suchlike, before finally tracking down a beatific Laura Bush clutching the new arrival. Goebbels would have been proud.

'Hijack Live' disappeared along with the cathode ray tube as a brick was flung at the television, and so the hijack's merciful anticlimax – and the inevitable studio debriefing – went unseen. One assumes the anchorman walked us through surrender with a large piece of Fuzzyfelt and some magic markers, before Sky's political analysts put the whole affair in context: the two Albanians on the bus were disguised Tory MPs, funded by Euro-poofs and Al-Qaeda zillionaires, trying to get fox-hunting reintroduced in the UK.

But as usual the truth is far simpler. That the hijackers demanded a flight to Russia is coincidental – it could have been anywhere. They had simply, belatedly, been confronted by the realities of the Athenian traffic system, and realised that they could die either by police sniper, or of old age on a congested overpass.

Greek police claimed the bloodless conclusion as a triumph of training over, it was implied, the traditional trigger-happiness and penchant for overkill of anti-terrorism forces east of Rome. Indeed, had the Olympics not shunted Greece from the seventeenth to the nineteenth century in terms of crowd control, the Albanians and their captives could well have found themselves up against the sort of logic once used by the medieval abbot of Citeaux: kill them all, God will know His own.

When it comes to soccer crowds, God searches in vain, a fact that is certain to be driven home at the end of a tyre-iron at some stage during the 2010 World Cup. In fact one hopes our own security forces are hard at work bayoneting sandbags and skipping through orange cones, or whatever it is that police and paramilitaries do when preparing to rough people up.

Why so *kragdadig*? Why worry when the rugby and cricket equivalents went off so well; when the only hooliganism seen at either came from hotel waitresses and advocates moonlighting as cricket administrators?

Simple. Those were entirely different ballgames. Besides, in 1995 white people were too afraid to misbehave lest Madiba change his mind and start a one-way ferry service to Robben Island: one peep from you lot, and the only thing Francois Pienaar's going to be lifting over his head is a pickaxe. Likewise, the prospect of cricket fans running amok is more endearing than alarming, rather like the elderly wife of a rural Anglican minister trying to beat a cockroach to death with a large ball of yarn.

No, something wicked this way comes, and it will be fascinating to watch liberal politicians and reformed security forces fight the urge to turn back the clock twenty years, to send out phalanxes of slit-eyed blond men with bristling moustaches. But old habits die hard.

Right, you bladdy boggers, come yere with your moffie haircut and your Soutie communist kak, and let's see who's hard and who isn't …

Merry sport of minstrelsy

When it's Niewe Djaar in Cape Town, Twiede Niewe Djaar must be around the corner. Or Derde, depending on one's work ethic. (Given the clandestine, whispered compliments from coloured Capetonians this elicited, I think it's high time someone founded Klopse Haters Anonymous.)

The Cape Town minstrels have a special place in the hearts of Capetonians. I think it's somewhere near the aortal valve. The doctors say it's too dangerous to operate, so there they stay.

They were once called Coons, but mercifully the vast lies that are racial stereotyping are a thing of the past. After ten years of democracy we are free to call the Cape minstrels what they are: tone-deaf sequined horrors of sartorial ghastliness, spangled harpies hell-bent on dragging an entire city into their annual quagmire of mindless, pointless, endless jollity. I don't like the minstrels.

But that's okay, because they don't like me. That's because I'm a white piece of shit. Or was it a piece of white shit? I forget: the day was hot, the traffic intersection was busy, and the men who dubbed me thus had terribly few teeth. But certainly albino faeces were involved after the pair of merry minstrels asked me at a traffic light to sponsor them R10 for transport and I declined.

For a moment one wondered what Scandinavian tourists would think of such an exhortation, especially having just read in their guidebook that the Cape Malays (found between

Cape Cobras and Cape Wangai Orang-utans) are cheeky but warm-hearted.

However, there was no need for concern. Dental catastrophe and its mesmerising effects on human speech would have left our valued visitors certain that two men in polystyrene boaters and cardboard spats had just bestowed upon them the Peace of Weitsit.

Still, one had to wonder how much dung was flung when the minstrels' request for ten million rands from the Western Cape government was turned down. In the end they had to settle for a measly two million, and complained bitterly to SABC's Charl Pauw that they'd had to spend 'millions to give the citizens of Cape Town a free show'. Them plastic ukuleles don't come cheap.

But more hardships were to come. With 2 January falling on Sunday this year, they were forced to take Monday off work to give the citizens of Cape Town the above-mentioned free show. You just can't expect artists to work like this.

A burning sense of self-righteous entitlement; an entrenched belief that frivolous self-gratification qualifies as a spectacle worth watching; an aggressive assertion of partying as culture; horrible music; ugly uniforms; the smell of slightly burnt boerewors rolls hanging over the baking asphalt: has the minstrels' parade finally become a fully-fledged South African sport?

It's always been competitive: teams are judged on apparel, musical skill, the length of their tongues and whether or not their backer is a major Cape Flats crime lord. But surely it is time for the organisers (if such a word is applicable to an event that generally unfolds like a fire in a kindergarten) to realise the fiscal possibilities of selling themselves and their grand traditions to someone like SuperSport?

I, for one, would be fascinated to watch the single-string banjo duel for men over 65, in which competitors improvise up to three variations on a short musical phrase ('Tjakkalang tjakkalang tjakkalay'). Synchronised parasol-dropping; the 10 km aimless meander; endurance-waiting (where the hell are those buses?); all are no less watchable than golf or swimming or a root canal performed in a Rawalpindi meat market with a nineteenth-century hand bore. With television money behind it, the parade could even expand to include real minstrels, people able to hold not only a genuine note, but hold it at the same instant as those around them.

Sport is culture, and eventually, as the fetish of inclusiveness takes hold, culture will be sport. It's a small step from Olympic curling to Olympic knitting, and a smaller one to Olympic hat-tipping and gold-tooth-flashing. Will the 2040 Games, held in Zumaville (formerly Benoni), see a Cape contingent go head to head with a posse of Swiss yodellers? If the minstrel organisers get organised, yes. Will I be there? I'd rather eat ground glass. Tjakkalang.

Loyal to what end?

As Mark Thatcher slithered away from a media frenzy, Prince Harry goose-stepped straight into another one. And back at home good men fell through the cracks, and nobody seemed to notice.

A poll conducted late last year by the BBC found that 50 per cent of Britons don't know about Auschwitz. In other words, Prince William knows about the extermination camps, Prince Harry doesn't. Charles knows, Fergie doesn't. Baroness Thatcher knows, Mark did but cut a deal and now he doesn't.

But Fergie does know other things. 'I know what it is like to have very bad press and be continuously criticised,' the Duchess said at the weekend, in defence of her thick swastika-wearing nephew-in-law. 'It is very tiring and unpleasant.' One must bear in mind that, to gals like Ferg, 'very tiring and unpleasant' also includes making toast and doing their own nails, but perhaps her irritation is not misplaced.

After all, Harry is no more of a genetically lobotomised lout than millions of other Britons, and *they're* not being carpeted. And besides, what better way for the royal family to accelerate its headlong rush into the open arms of populist mediocrity than by indulging in middle-class fantasies of latent anti-Semitic cruelty and kinky SS uniforms? Oh darling, you look hot in black, and those silver skulls really bring out the colour in your pimples …

Harry's costume was in poor taste, said the broadsheets, implying that gas chambers are a matter of taste. Luckily one could turn the page to the advertisements for accessories emblazoned with the hammer and sickle of the Soviet Union, that jagged motif that presided damply over the executions of twenty million innocent Russians. But if Joe Slovo has it on his tombstone, it must be okay.

Perhaps it was Harry and the Nazis. Perhaps it was Darfur. Perhaps it was the sixtieth anniversary of the liberation of Auschwitz. Or perhaps Sports Minister Makhenkesi Stofile is just dumber than a bag full of hammers. But whatever half-formed notions flitted through what we will, for the sake of charity, refer to as the Minister's brain, the result was a prediction that genocide was imminent in South African rugby.

'I told South African rugby that I was not amused by the latest developments in the sport,' he said last weekend, ruffling his petticoats and giving the Prince Regent a little kiss on the cheek, 'and will not tolerate any ethnic cleansing.'

One imagines the gathered press sat silent, trying to convince itself that no public figure could possibly be so stupid and insensitive as to compare race-based handbag-swinging between peevish and overpaid sports administrators with genocide. But the Minister plunged on.

'Rugby seems to be moving uncomfortably towards racial cleansing and this is what the country and the ministry of sport will not tolerate,' he said.

Admittedly it takes a rare and uncomplicated soul not to cherish thoughts of mass murder whenever South African rugby's boorish and fractious politburo undermine the happy game with vain posturing, paranoid sniping and rank incompetence; but Stofile has gone way, way too far. Forget Harry. If anyone should be made to visit a camp and undergo compulsory enrolment in Basic Humanity 101, it is Stofile.

But Stofile isn't alone. Rugby and basic humanity parted company years ago, when little boys stopped playing barefoot and flyhalves stopped going home to their real jobs. And one can't help feeling that Dale McDermott was a victim of that human void.

His suicide was newsworthy enough to make newspaper placards around the country, but its causes, and its implications, have been almost entirely ignored. A single obituary in a Sunday newspaper marked his passing; a website rehashed an earlier favourable piece about him.

It would be dangerous – and hurtful to his family – to indulge in amateur psychology, to pin his death on the awful macho insularity of Afrikaner rugby. After all, he had a history of depression that predated his association with the Springboks.

But it must have been an awful realisation for him when, having summoned the courage to blow the whistle on Kamp Staaldraad – the embodiment of all the ugly, frightened, brutalised and brutalising beliefs ingrained in the sport – he saw that he was going to be ignored by Jake White's new administration; that the cancer remained.

At the time, Joost van der Westhuizen called him 'Judas'. At least we know Joost has read one book, although it's possible he just got told what happens at the end. The irony of citing a Christian text to condemn a reformer was no doubt utterly lost on Van der Westhuizen.

McDermott's mother said her son remained loyal to Springbok rugby until the end. One wonders why.

Say goodbye to the games we knew

Every so often, grumpy white readers would tell me not to mix sport and politics, which confirmed for me that newspapers and glasses of Klippies and Coke shouldn't be mixed either.

Sports fans who don't understand sport are like Labradors that won't stop humping your leg. Try as you might, you can't shake them off, and people around you start producing pinched little smiles and sidewise glances that imply you're doing something provocative. Stop flirting with the pooch, they seem to say.

Away you walk, dragging with you your hunk o' burning mutt-lust, and attempt to introduce a cosmopolitan boredom to the whole thing. Oh, *this* dog? You mean you don't have one yourself? Oh my darling, it's all the rage in Buenos Aires! Chihuahuas, you know. Three to a leg.

Of course those with no feeling for games tend to thrust themselves less at one's thighs than one's ears, but the sense of being molested by something bestial – and, more importantly, by something that can never achieve the satisfaction it so desperately seeks – remains. They rattle off chapter and verse, averages, names, dates. Everything about the wannabe is precise; except his teeth, which recall a collapsed heap of fossilised bones, as if the Diplodocus in the museum's main gallery had finally slipped its wires and succumbed to 65 million years of gravity.

To the white sports fan, knee still unencumbered by canine

suitors and so entirely free to jerk spasmodically at fresh news of quotas and political intervention, Butana Komphela must have seemed like the worst kind of mongrel gigolo after his pronouncements last week. Indeed, it was not only quotas on the agenda of the chairperson of Parliament's sport portfolio committee, but compulsory, universal, jackbooted quotas.

According to Mr Komphela, teams not fielding a fully representative mix would be nailed, with punishments including withdrawing the right to use the South African flag.

'When they are not reflective of the democracy of our country, they can't take anything South African,' he said.

But reactionary barbs about politics and sport not mixing are unfounded here. The ANC politicians calling for transformation and quotas are not doing so out of schadenfreude or a perverse desire to see Apartheid emblems like the Springbok dragged through the mud. They don't sit around at night stroking Fu Manchu beards, plotting new ways to irritate the white bourgeoisie. They have given this plenty of thought, negotiated conflicting and mutually exclusive positions, and made a tough executive decision that they believed to be in the best interests of South Africa.

Because that's what nationalists do, especially those weaned on poverty, socialism and Marxism. They honestly don't know that sport isn't the Marshall Plan, that it is a wretchedly thin foundation for social engineering. And somewhere they've forgotten that sport represents everything liberation struggles try to destroy.

Sport is elitist. Anyone who wants to argue that toss needs to go two rounds with a pro fighter, and then we'll see if fuzzy notions of universal brotherhood persist. Sport is imperialistic: territory is gained by force or guile, and there's no prize for coming second. It tolerates no affirmative action. Those who are up to its challenges are affirmed; the rest are crushed like the no-hopers and also-rans they always were. It defies and denies intellectualism and theorising. It idolises class hierarchy, as nimble backline toffs with clean jerseys keep upwind of forelock-tugging forwards with their webbed toes.

But most of all, it serves no utilitarian purpose. You get fitter filling sandbags or digging mass graves. There's more fun to be had in sex or cow-tipping. As a nation-building tool it comes a very distant third behind war and explicit propaganda. And it makes considerably less money than pharmaceuticals and arms.

But let's play the representivity game. Let's be 'reflective of the democracy of our country'. Are we to include six women in every cricket team? Should we reflect that between 10 and 25 per cent of the country is HIV-positive; that one in three South African men are obese? And let's not forget that 40 per cent of the population is under 18. Are we looking at a Springbok team containing various permutations of six teenagers, five blobs, and two cases of HIV infection?

Of course not, because the politicians aren't talking about true representivity. Theirs is a grander vision, of sport as social force. If social engineering is what South Africa needs, then all power to them. If this will raise the majority from poverty, and instil a sense of self-worth in the masses, then legislated transformation is worth a try.

But first let's pause to bid farewell to the games we knew. And let's be clear about whose best interests we have at heart.

Great white hope

In which Spade and Crunchy open a can of whupass and a can of worms at the same time.

In the words of Bobby Kennedy, there's nothing like a good old-fashioned no-holds-barred race riot. No sir, said Bobby one day while we were dynamiting for trout in the Oswald Pirow Dam, you can't beat watching tolerance-mongering New Englanders give in to the overwhelming urge to leave tyre-iron-shaped depressions in 'fros, or iron-willed Nation of Islam acolytes renouncing their pacifism just long enough to perform avant-garde rhinoplasties on smug beaky Caucasian noses with baseball bats.

Not that Bobby would ever take part in such barbarism, mind you. He understands that violence inspired by racial intolerance is a stain on humanity and besmirches the other, far more honourable, motives for violence, such as oil, land, water, religion, and the slope of eyelids. Indeed, it has also curtailed by association all violence inspired by racial tolerance, derailing many admirable ambitions to invade and annihilate aggressively sanctimonious countries such as Belgium and the Netherlands. Not that one should need an excuse to obliterate Belgium, but one doesn't want to be called a racist when the napalm canisters start raining down on Brussels.

No, what Bobby means is that race-based hoedowns have always been with us, and since they're a fact of life, one should take advantage of them as spectator sports. And Boxing South

Africa agrees entirely. This week it revealed that black-versus-white bouts put bums on seats like nothing else, and bemoaned the dearth of toned white bums being put on the canvas by beefy black champions.

But what do the fans really want when they demand black–white bouts? Are they interested in contrasting styles, or are they getting a tiny vicarious race-riot kick? And if it's the latter, why box at all? Why not formalise and contain the whole thing by simply putting two blokes in a ring and handing them microphones? And why not go the whole hog, rolling out a farm-fresh white boy with sandy moustache, watery blue eyes and shorts worn under his armpits, to face up to a gunmetal-blue bro from the projects, 'fro standing up like an Ethiopian space helmet, his banter quick and deadly as an AK?

'Ladiss and jennilmin! In the white corner, weighing in at 120 kilograms, nursing a chip on his shoulder and favouring the right, it's Gerrrrrie "Crunchy" Poggenpoooooooel! Annnndinow, in the black corner, weighing in at 121 kilograms, sporting a previous disadvantage and able to flip-flop between his left and right depending on prevailing economic policies, it's Sipho "Spade" Vilakaaaaaazi!'

Crunchy gets in the first jab. 'Blacks always walk in the road with their backs to oncoming traffic and then get a huge fright when you hoot, as if the last thing they're expecting is car.'

A cut opens up over Spade's eyes, but he rallies. 'Whites always wipe their hand on their pants when you've shaken it.'

'Blacks don't understand queues.'

'Whites don't understand Ubuntu. You don't need queues with Ubuntu.'

'Blacks can't define Ubuntu, which is very convenient for point-scoring rhetoric.'

'Whites can't understand Ubuntu because they're not African.'

'Not African? We've been here for 350 years! That's ten generations. That's eight generations more than a lot of Indians, who call themselves black.'

'And in ten generations you couldn't get around to learning a single indigenous language?' Crunchy goes down in a heap, and the crowd gasps. The fighters retreat to their corners, revived respectively with biltong and samp. Round two ...

'Blacks blame their helplessness on Apartheid.'

'You mean the regime that whites didn't vote for or endorse? Whites blame everything on blacks blaming everything on Apartheid.' A cautionary word from the ref – wise-ass conundrums will not be tolerated. Another angle is required. 'Whites have horrible dress sense and no innate style.' Crunchy reels, clutching at his long sideburns and handlebar moustache as his head rings.

'Blacks all have little scars on their shins that look like cigarette burns.'

'Bald whites look like butternuts. Bald blacks look like supermodels. And speaking of which, whites don't have shoulders or stomach muscles.'

'At least we've got calf muscles.' A gasp from the crowd as Spade's knee buckles.

'B-blacks can harmonise,' he gasps.

'Ja, because all traditional black music is in C major and a combination of five notes. White music is Mozart, Bach, the Beatles. White music is bliss.'

'Bru,' says Vilakazi, and the stadium falls silent. 'Five words: Helmut Lotti, Liberace, Richard Clayderman.'

Crunchy hits the canvass like a sack of koeksisters. It's all over.

You'll never walk again

In which the 82nd Airborne Division is given a run for its money.

Those who attack American interests around the globe, who incite peaceful native populations to fanaticism and violence, and who undermine democracy must expect swift and decisive action by the United States and its military. This was the word from US Secretary of State Condoleezza Rice on Friday as she outlined her country's plans to invade Manchester.

While Rice said it was too early to include the English city in a 'redefined axis, or maybe a parallelogram, of evil', she confirmed that the 82nd Airborne Division had set up an operations centre in Liverpool, from where it would carry out what Pentagon sources are calling 'Operation Fiscal Valor'.

'At this stage our strategy revolves around ballistic pacification options,' said Rice. 'An initial aerial suppression blanket will be rolled out, consisting of temperature-enhancing incendiary democracy-clusters and laser-guided tyranny-dismantlers with special "Free to bear arms if you've still got arms" ball-bearing spray pattern. Any unscheduled enemy precocity in the arena of survival will be absorbed by life-cessation manoeuvres by Special Forces sanitation teams equipped with low-environmental-impact ordnance, such as bicycle chains and straight-razors, which do away with demoralising ballistics evidence.'

Earlier in the week President George W Bush told Congress that the burning of an American flag by Manchester youths – clad in the traditional red football shirts indicating their allegiance to local strongman 'Sir' Alex Ferguson – was an affront to the sovereignty and values of the moral majority of Americans.

'This world is not our world,' said Bush, whose ten-minute address was characterised by prolonged applause from delegates and whose frequent pauses, illustrated with a half smile and short snorts, contributed to an overwhelming sense of a punchline deferred. 'The green and pleasant land once described by the poet Maya Angelou is gone, replaced by the satanic mills of tyranny. These terrorists who trample our dignity hate our freedom. They hate our Astroturf. They hate the bounty of gridiron football, where points flow as freely as the milk from the breast of a 19-year-old Iowan cheerleader nursing blonde triplets. They want to destroy all the treasures the United States has given to the Briddish over the centuries: railways, policing, universities, democracy, Christianity, the English language, Elizabeth Taylor.'

Meanwhile Manchester militias, recently joined under the banner of 'Manchester United', have been bracing for a backlash after booing American tycoon Malcolm Glazer, who is set to buy a controlling share in the local oil industry. The city produces over three barrels of oil a week, mostly as a by-product of its ancient fish-and-chips industry, although smaller refineries also process the facial cotton swabs discarded by spotty teenagers, extracting up to half a barrel a week.

In a secret underground locker room in Old Trafford, Manchester United leadership was upbeat about its chances of seeing off an American attack.

'Mareens? Boonch of pufes,' said one Barry Smith, his head wrapped in a long red scarf with eyeholes cut in it. 'Tooking dere trousers into dere butes like dat. Lukes daft. And dat dere Chorj Boosh, eez crap.'

Tony and Gary Smith, cousins of Barry, concur. 'Really really crap like. Eez ommost as crap as Tony Bleh. And *eez* really crap. Cyant hold is drink like. Pufe. Now dat Ronnie Rehgan, ee was hahd like. Hahd as iron. Weda had Ronnie Rehgan down ere any time, oop inda terraces like at da footy.'

Did they think Ronald Reagan's administration might have reacted differently to their objections to Glazer's takeover?

'Dum reet he woulda!' they declare nostalgically. 'He woulda nooked us feh joost looching a' him squint! Tha's how hahd Ronnie Rehgan was. Hahd and devilish handsome. Not leek dis pufe Boosh. Yev got to be hahd but feh.'

'Hahd boot feh,' agrees an anonymous youth, strapping plastic bottles of ale to himself. He and his ilk have been attacking American tourists all week in an orchestrated campaign of irritation. Entering crowded backpackers' lodges undetected, these desperate freedom fighters quickly quaff all nine or ten bottles on their person, triggering tremendous attacks of vomiting and maudlin singing.

'Hahd boot feh,' he repeats. 'Lahk me dud. Used to thrash me evertime Liverpule beat oos. Said life were aboot hahd knocks and drinkin' like, an ee were reet. Miserable dead bastard pufe. Miss im like buggery, though.'

At the time of going to print, network executives had not yet confirmed whether the war would start on cable during the half-time break of the Dallas–Steelers game, or whether it would be confined to NBC and CBS, between *Will and Grace* and *Everybody Loves Raymond*.

Park of Darkness

A pathetically thin excuse for publicising my Newlands debut. Still, not as thin as my forward defensive, which proved my undoing after ten gloriously purloined runs.

The fag-end of a Cape Town summer is a bad-tempered swelter. The heat is frayed, its December esprit evaporated with the ice cream and tourists. What remains is an exhausted, impatient shimmer of cracking tar and acres of council-planted kindling. The sea is a dirty green and blotched with sharks scuffing past one another as their dorsal fins blister and peel in the sun. The Scandinavian backpackers in Long Street have dirty toenails and the thousand-yard stares of people casting off from reality, slowly forgetting Oslo, careers and mortgages as cheap dagga and suffocating nights in grubby hostels pick at the hinges of their consciousness.

On Sunday I took a slow boat through the choked backwaters of that sluggish, steaming, backward city. There was no sound save the occasional screech of a Maltese poodle being caught in an automatic garage door. The captain began firing the forward 10-pounder into the tree line. We thought we saw shapes capering in the primordial undergrowth, perhaps ADT guards interrupted halfway through their midmorning Gatsby. The tar was black and oily, a river of molasses leading us deeper into the white heart of the Newlands.

Some tributaries were entirely blocked. The drums beat on, bringing reports from the north that a group of cyclists, acolytes of the masochistic Velocipede Brotherhood, were pushing on into the jaws of the south-easter, the wind keeping them on the spot like 35 000 hamsters in pink Spandex hurtling towards oblivion on the great exercise wheel of testicular doom. Later we passed a huddle of the feral dachshunds that haunted these parts, squabbling over the remains of a rider who had wandered from the pack. We saw a shoe, a fingerless glove, a tibia. The dogs snarled and tried to give chase, but their legs were too short and their bellies dragged on the pavement.

Newlands Cricket Ground (or, as it is now called, Shariah Park Newlands, or something equally incongruous and prescriptive) is a terribly sad place in mid-March. The divots gaily ploughed by international kneecaps a month ago have baked hard into tiny saucer-sized salt pans, and the awnings of the Railway Stand flap wanly, like the sails of a typhoid-ravaged schooner becalmed in the Sargasso.

All of which went unnoticed by the Wellhungovers and the Cape Town Big Boys XI as they squared up, twelve against thirteen, for a social thrash in front of 25 000 empty, echoing seats. Miles away, at least two Capetonian columnists fought nappy rash on Suikerbossie and swore at every rider who struggled past them with a cheery word about the difficulties of writing something funny about the Argus. But some of us pick our ordeals with more discretion, and, marking out a run-up at the Kelvin Grove end, as tumbleweed rolled in from extra cover, one couldn't help smirking in a self-satisfied way.

But two hours at fine leg, with dust drifting into fine dunes around one's shins, tends to shift smiles to the other side of one's face (the lee side, the side not having flakes of irradiated skin blown off it by the gale). Fortunately there are always those less fortunate than ourselves to observe, who give us perspective on our own misery. And up in the deserted darkness of the President's Pavilion sat the official scorer in her lonely hutch, haemorrhaging away a Sunday she will never get back, so that we might know that the current run rate was 1.23 per over, and that Muggins's two runs had been scored backward of square (both deflections off his chin) and had been 32 minutes in the making. Her little pale face bobbed in the window far away as she desperately tried to hear the bowler's name in the wind.

'Huuuur!' the skipper seemed to be bellowing, impatiently gesturing at his seamer, as if she had somehow managed to misidentify Shane Warne. 'Huuuur!'

'Herbert?' she yelled back, her voice cracking.

'No! Mnyuuuur!'

'His name is Ginuuur!' screamed extra cover, to speed up the process.

'Geniel?' She felt her larynx rupture. Rolled eyes, despairing hands thrown into the air.

The captain began a long-suffering trudge towards the stands, and climbed, hands on knees, to her cubby hole. 'The bowler is Smith. Okay? Smith. Would you like me to spell that for you?'

We never found out her name. Like the angel she was, she disappeared into the ether as soon as the last wide had been rebowled, the last leg-bye limped.

And we wretches dispersed into the gathering gloom.

101 Ways to End Your Career

I'd wanted to go out in style on 100 columns but, true to the cavalier spirit of the column, had miscounted. It's peculiar saying goodbye to readers who you aren't entirely convinced existed in the first place. Writing a column is like performing standup in front of a very dark, very silent theatre: without the odd piece of hate-mail – and the odder piece of fan mail – it might seem that one is entirely alone. Still, it was fun while it lasted.

Sports journalism is an oxymoron. I'm not being unkind by saying so. Find a sports journalist, perhaps sleeping under a pool table on the East Rand, the widening moat of drool spreading under his unshaven cheek reflecting the pole-dancer's neon panties. Grab him by the lapels of his grey patched-patent-leather jacket, and haul him to his feet. Make sure his *faux* alligator-hide loafers with crepe soles don't slip out from under him. Peel the Lucky Strike from behind his ear and light it for him. Then ask him what he does for a living.

Brain surgeon, he'll say. He'll laugh, and shudder. Then he'll remember where he is. What kind of a bloody ignorant thing is that to ask, he'll say, and stumble for the door.

Of course there are some sports writers who are proud of their profession, who look out across the tented field with a beatific half-smile, who greet their colleagues with a serene nod. Their shirts are pressed and they eat their lunch with cutlery rather than fingers. They believe that sport is about merit and competition, that one day they'll wake up to discover that transformation and those awful uppity black politicians have all been a bad dream. They don't know that their wives are slowly warming to erotic asphyxiation techniques, and that purported book-club get-togethers have long since devolved into squeaking, ripping, popping orgies of black latex and vacuum masks. And they don't know that their manly colleagues, those fellows they hail so cheerily, call them things like Molly and Soggy Biscuit, and construct terribly cruel narratives about them, the kind that only bored young men with some literary ability and few scruples can concoct.

But at least this savage band of slackers who saves its creativity for press-box character assassination knows that it is degenerate. It knows that when it is mentioned at family functions its mother smiles anxiously and asks if the food is still warm enough, that its father crumples his serviette under the table in agonies of poker-faced shame. Because nobody studies sports journalism: press boxes around the world are full of half-finished degrees in geology and sociology, of recently resigned schoolteachers and jaded club coaches, of former players and also-rans rapidly subsiding into sad autumnal lives of fat and knee operations and obscurity.

Perhaps editors have given sports journalism this inferiority complex, seeing the back pages as a sordid commercial necessity that helps pay for the noble front pages in which wormy cans are opened and clay feet are revealed. Perhaps it's the reporter's own guilt at being paid to report in dull journalese the details of a game that his readers watched with surround-sound and action replays. Perhaps it's simply a function of being assimilated into the retinues of international stars en route to clubs and being asked by pretty girls for an autograph, and having to shout admissions (to be heard about the music) that render you irrelevant in their world view. There's nothing like screaming 'I'm not famous! I'm nobody!' at three beautifully groomed soccer-moms-to-be to put one in touch with one's basic humanity.

Why do they go on? Free chocolate éclairs, for one thing. But maybe they go on because they don't know how to stop. It's simply too hard to think about picking up third-year criminology courses when you could just wait for the Tri-Nations to start. And besides, they've watched enough grand sendoffs to harbour secret fantasies about getting on themselves.

They've disguised the frogs in their throats with jocular comments as retiring giants walked off the field in tears under a deluge of applause and rose petals or strode away towards the dressing-room with chins held high, their team mates forming an honour-guard with cricket bats aloft. They've lauded the greats for quitting while they were ahead, and gone home to stare at the wall and reflect on thirty more years of vicarious pleasure. Their quitting points have come and gone, and they're in it for life.

But sometimes they do notice the quitting points. In the two years since the debut of this column I've been called a racist, a homophobe, a traitor, an idiot (oh when will sports fans buy thesauruses?), and a bitch; and perhaps that last epithet is worth developing: 101 little journalistic Dalmatians – spotted, blotchy, not black but not entirely white either – have entered the world as *Pitch&Mutters*.

And that, I think, is enough for this bitch.

The Contented Loneliness of
the Late-Afternoon Net-Bowler

This was written for an 'M&G' supplement that never happened, and for a while I was relieved. I'd been asked to write about 'My Sporting Passion', but I worried that the brash garrulity of the 'Pitch&Mutter' would drown out this little meditation, this little flash of honesty; and it was easiest to let it disappear unmolested. Besides, 'passion' is too noisy an idea to describe what so many of us feel about the sports we admire. But now it seems fitting to give this piece the last word, after all the sound and fury.

The inexpert sportsman is sustained by fantasy. A stranger to those thrills so casually, so wastefully, enjoyed by more gifted players of games, he compensates for the hours of boredom spent on the bench or at deep third man by imagining. Sometimes, when sitters have been dropped or shoelaces tripped over, or batting partners run out for absolutely no reason other than that it was time to take a quick one, despite having padded the ball straight to silly mid-off, the mind is the only refuge.

For the inexpert cricketer, teams are tiresome and excessively concrete encumbrances, filled with cheerful, dim lads, their skill and cheerfulness apparently directly proportionate to their dimness. An unexceptional pun from the night before is strangled to death across a session, like a frog being killed by boys gradually becoming bored with their sadism. The sweating man at midwicket claps incessantly, a wind-up toy for imbecile babies, his tongue always visible. In the afternoon his claps begin to sound like gunshots, perhaps muffled by virtue of the muzzle pressing against something. Something like the back of his head, perhaps.

And yet the inexpert sportsman, a cricketer in this case, always comes back to the game, always hopes for the best, always smells freshly cut grass and dew on leaves whenever the game is mentioned.

It is solitude that brings me back. The nets I use are tucked away in a corner of a school's grounds, surrendered to Under-15 teams and the enormous droppings of roving golden retrievers, and the concrete does terrible things to cricket balls. But in the last act of a perfect Cape day, with Egyptian geese flirting garrulously overhead and the dying wind slipping through and around the row of plane trees, there is nothing that brings me closer to that unreachable thing that one looks for in calm moments, alone, outdoors, when the day is over.

Of course reality often intrudes. An unplanned leg-cutter hits a ragged tear in the felt and disappears through a hole in the side of the net, scudding across a road to be entombed forever by ivy. An obsessive-compulsive border collie makes the ball the centre of its palpitating universe, and I am forced to play Elmer Fudd to its Bugs Bunny. I have found that collie spit often makes the ball squat a little.

And then there are the little boys, old enough to want to prove themselves against a Real Left-Arm Seamer who stands three feet taller than them, but young enough to hesitate and blush and ask, without posturing, if I would bowl at them. Invariably one of them owns a celestial cover-drive. Nothing else, to be sure, but it's worth bowling full and wide to watch that shot, and the overly-focused, almost sanctimonious expression of a boy trying not to look as proud as he feels.

But mostly it's just the net and the afternoon and me, and the deeply satisfying irritations of uncontrolled swing, of hitting off-stump with a clang (and so missing out on the pleasing commotion of the ball as it surges up into the netting behind). Apparently when expert bowlers run in, they think of where to land the ball, or else they think of nothing. I am not an expert bowler, and so I think of many things, like wondering how old Heather Locklear really is, or considering the financial pros and cons of starting my own mulberry-bottling business.

Sporting fantasies rarely intrude. I have no desire to take a hat trick at the MCG, because as much as I respect Graeme Smith and Jacques Kallis, I don't want them rushing at me to ruffle my hair and touch my bottom. But Heather Locklear and mulberries somehow gain a profundity as the last sun fades from the tops of the planes, and each ball – hup, oof, swish, thwack – seems to bring me closer to seeing a pattern, a truth.

And then it's home in the still, warm half-dark, and back to the world.

Acknowledgements

These columns would never have seen daylight without the support and encouragement of Julia Beffon, the tireless sports editor of the *Mail&Guardian*, whose sense of humour and patience allowed me to call myself a sports writer without ever having to write about sport.